PIONEER CHILDREN

True Tales of the Old West

by

Charles L. Convis

Watercolor Cover by Mary Anne Convis

PIONEER PRESS, CARSON CITY, NEVADA

Library of Congress Catalog Card Number: 96-68502
742 8339
ISBN 1-892156-10-5

Printed by
KNI, Incorporated
Anaheim, California

CONTENTS

ILLUSTRATIONS

THE SAGER ORPHANS

Henry Sager, a restless man, kept moving west. When he reached St. Joseph, Missouri, he decided to move on to Oregon. Naomi tried to stop him. They had six children, and she was expecting the seventh.

"I'll never make it, Henry," she protested. "I'll never live to see Oregon."

But Henry, like many others, had Oregon fever. In that year of 1844, fifteen hundred emigrants followed the trail of Marcus and Narcissa Whitman, laid down eight years before. The Sagers joined the company led by William Shaw. John, thirteen, and Francis, eleven, helped herd the spare oxen and cattle. Catherine, nine, Elizabeth, seven, and Matilda, five, helped their mother and three-year-old Louise.

On May 30, while camped in a thunderstorm, Naomi had another girl, Rosanna. The difficult birth left Naomi so weak the company waited three days before moving on.

Hard luck continued. On July 30 the Sager wagon ran over Catherine's lower leg, breaking both bones. Henry set the bones as best he could, and Catherine was put in the wagon bed with her mother and the new baby.

Henry Sager was sick with typhoid when they moved through South Pass on August 23. Too weak to walk, he rode in his wagon. Three days later he called for the captain. Shaw had to bend low to hear Henry's whisper:

"I ain't gonna make it, captain. I'd be obliged if you'd see my family through to the Whitman Mission." He died minutes later.

Naomi had never recovered from the childbirth. With Henry gone, she sank into delirium before they reached Fort Hall. Catherine remembered the choking dust of the trail, the stifling, jolting wagon, and her mother's piteous cries. Naomi died on September 11, sixteen days after Henry. Rosanna was taken by a woman who had breast milk.

The wagon train reached the Whitman mission in late October. Catherine remembered the modest Whitman cabin as something palatial. When Captain Shaw walked inside to talk to Narcissa Whitman, both Sager boys finally expecting help in the heavy responsibility of five younger sisters, broke down and cried. The four girls looked from their brothers to the cabin, wondering what would happen next.

Captain Shaw and Narcissa came outside. The girls looked at each other and held their breath. They heard the captain ask if she had any children.

Narcissa pointed to a grave at the foot of a nearby hill. "The only child I ever had sleeps there," she said. "It's a great comfort to be able to see her grave from the house." She looked back at the captain. "But if the Lord casts these little ones upon us, He will give us His grace and strength to do our duty." She turned to the children. "Come, boys. Get your sisters' bonnets and come inside so we can have a look at you."

Three days later the wagon with baby Rosanna and her wet nurse reached the mission. Rosanna was five months old, but no larger than a three -weeks-old baby.

For the next few days, the Sager children listened to the adults discuss what should be done. The Whitmans were already raising Mary Ann Bridger and Helen Meek, half-Indian daughters of two mountain men. They decided to keep all the Sagers so they could stay together.

Catherine cried most of the first few weeks at the mission. Narcissa Whitman kept the children clean and fed, but Catherine still grieved for her parents. Her leg had not yet healed, so she could not join her brothers and sisters in exploring theie new home and the surrounding woods. She stayed indoors and sewed. She often rocked her baby sister, whose name had been changed to Henrietta to honor their parents.

The Whitmans had firm ideas about raising children. For the next three years the Sagers lived under strict rules, tempered with loving care. They helped with the housework and attended family worship every morning and evening. Each child learned a daily verse of scripture, and each tended a section of a large vegetable garden.

Catherine's leg healed, and she could walk about. She and her brothers and sisters and the Bridger and Meek girls enjoyed swimming, singing lessons, and long walks with Narcissa to study plant life.

The children grew to love the Whitmans, calling them mother and father. As the boys approached manhood, Marcus Whitman became their legal guardian.

The Whitmans had worked hard with the neighboring Cayuse Indians, teaching them agriculture, health, and religion. But an epidemic of measles in late 1847, brought by emigrant travelers, struck the Indians as well as the whites at the mission.

On November 29, sixteen-year-old John Sager and Mary Ann Bridger were helping Doctor Whitman in the kitchen when several angry Indians entered. The measles had killed three Indian children the night before. Even though Catherine and Louise Sager and Helen Meek were also ill, the Indians blamed the epidemic on Whitman.

The Indians struck Doctor Whitman from behind with an axe. He fell to the floor, mortally wounded. John grabbed a pistol and fired twice. He hit two Indians before he was shot in the neck. Mary Ann ran to tell Narcissa that her husband and John had been killed.

The Indians, now on a rampage, shot and killed Narcissa. Fifteen-year-old Francis helped Matilda and other children into an attic room. He knelt and quickly prayed that God would save them. Then he ran to look for John. Just as he found his brother, Francis, too, was shot. He fell dead across John's body.

Catherine led her other sisters and the two half-Indian girls into an attic room. Sick herself, she stayed up all night with the others, trying to calm their fears and her own. The night was filled with shrieks and wails from Indians and whites, alike. All the Indian women and most of the men deplored what a small minority of their tribe had done. When the carnage ended, nine persons were dead, six men, Narcissa, and the Sager boys.

Within a week, death from measles claimed Helen Meek and Louise Sager. Mary Ann Bridger died a few days later. The four remaining Sager girls were now orphaned for the second time in their young lives.

In addition to grieving the loss of their adopted parents and their three siblings, the four Sager girls had been captured by the Indians.

A few weeks later, Peter Skene Ogden, a representative of the Hudson's Bay Company, bought the captives from the Cayuses with a large load of blankets, clothing, guns, and ammunition. He sent them to Oregon City at the end of the Oregon Trail, which had been the Sager's original destination when they left St. Joseph.

The four Sager girls were placed in separate homes among the settlers. Elizabeth and Henrietta were moved from family to family several times. Matilda and Catherine found more permanent homes.

Thirteen-year-old Catherine lived with the superintendent of a Methodist mission, and appreciated the home life he and his wife provided. Three years later she married Clark Pringle, who became a Methodist circuit rider. The couple had Elizabeth and Henrietta come live with them. Matilda was two days' travel away.

Catherine and Clark had eight children. When she realized that her childhood memories, horrible as they were, would help illuminate important events in history, Catherine began giving talks around the Pacific Northwest. This tiny, frail-looking woman was honored and respected as a strong, courageous, and resilient pioneer.

Suggested reading: Clifford M. Drury, *Marcus and Narcissa Whitman and the Opening of old Oregon* (Glendale: Arthur Clark Co., 1973).

CATHERINE SAGER PRINGLE

Oregon Historical Society

NO APOLOGIES

When Fred Lockley interviewed Matilda Sager Delaney in Oregon on Christmas Eve, 1921, she said, " My childhood was a time of terror. They say I am hard and bitter."

Matilda was four when her parents left Missouri for Oregon in 1844. After her parents died of typhoid fever on the journey, the seven Sager orphans were left with Marcus and Narcissa Whitman at their Waiilatpu Mission near the Columbia River.

Three years later Matilda lost her older brothers in the Cayuse Indian massacre at the mission. Matilda and her four sisters were captured. One of the sisters soon died of measles, although Matilda escaped the epidemic. Peter Skene Ogden purchased the other four sisters from the Indians, took them to Fort Walla Walla, and turned them over to Missionary Henry Spalding, who took them to Oregon City.

A preacher in Salem asked for the oldest Sager girl, thirteen-year-old Catherine; she would be the most useful. Spalding insisted that the preacher also take Henrietta, the youngest, the one born on the trail west.

Henrietta was passed on from family to family. Matilda heard she was taken to California. Later she learned that Henrietta had been killed, but she never learned any details.

Matilda, eight, was given to a farm family near Forest Grove, Oregon. From then until she married, Matilda was whipped so much she came to think of it like the winter rain — inevitable, to be borne without complaint.

One day Matilda's foster father saddled his horse and told the girl to bring a thick switch. She cut one and brought it, thinking it was for the horse. The man took the whip and beat her unmercifully.

"What have I done?" screamed the bewildered girl.

"You haven't done anything," he replied. "But I'm going away. Chances are you will do something to deserve a beating while I'm gone. I won't be here to give it to you, so I'm seeing to my duty before I leave."

The foster father was "intensely religious." He refused to let Matilda attend school, as he disagreed with the teacher on religious principles. He also refused to let Matilda go to church or Sunday School. His favorite bible verse was "spare the rod and spoil the child."

Matilda was whipped once for going to an entertainment at a local church. Her foster father said it was ungodly to seek worldly amusement; next she would want to go to a theater, and that was the gateway to hell and damnation.

He whipped Matilda for associating with a girl her own age. The girl had been born out of wedlock, and he did not consider her an appropriate companion for his foster daughter. When Matilda's forbidden friend was thirteen, she married a 35-year-old man. Within a year their cabin burned with the young bride in it. Her husband was hanged for the murder.

Matilda's foster father once took her to see a hanging.

"I want you to watch it," he said. "It will impress on your mind what happens to people who do not mind their elders and do exactly what they are told."

Matilda still remembered vividly the killing of the Whitmans and her brothers. Many months passed before she stopped having nightmares about the hanging.

"I could see him twitch with his tongue hanging out and his eyes protruding," she told Lockley.

Matilda remembered her foster mother walking the floor as she suffered from a toothache. It was cured when her husband knocked the tooth out of her head with a steel punch and hammer.

Neighbors eventually complained about so much whipping of Matilda. When she was taken before a judge, her foster father said the neighbors should mind their own business — he could discipline her more effectively if the judge would bind her out to him until she was sixteen. The judge was willing, but there was some dispute about her age.

When Matilda was fifteen, she married a 31-year-old miner from California. She went to the mines with him, and had five children in the next eight years. Her husband died, and she took in washing to support her family.

She married again and had three more children. A few years after her second husband died, she married for the third time.

Matilda was eighty-one when Lockley interviewed her. She did not apologize for being hard and bitter.

Suggested reading: Fred Lockley, *Conversations with Pioneer Women* (Eugene: Rainy Day Press, 1981).

NEVER TAKE NO CUTOFFS

When the family of thirteen-year-old Virginia Reed left Springfield, Illinois, in April, 1846 to travel to California, it went in style. Two of their ox-drawn wagons carried supplies. Virginia christened the third wagon the Pioneer Palace Car. It had cushioned seats, both heating and cooking stoves, a library, a side entrance, and a second story for sleeping. The wealthy Reeds even took a maid to care for Virginia's grandmother. Virginia's mother was in poor health, almost an invalid.

James Reed wanted to be Indian Agent for all the country west of the Rocky Mountains. He hoped the rising political fortunes of neighbor, Abraham Lincoln, would help.

Virginia had her own pony, Billy. She rode him every day. After they reached California, she wrote back to a cousin in Springfield, saying they left full of hope and did not dream of sorrow.

Bad luck came quickly. The emigrants buried Virginia's mother beside the trail in Kansas. The Reeds lost their best oxen just west of South Pass in Wyoming. By this time other emigrant trains had joined the Reed-Donner train. Lansford Hastings suggested they leave the well-traveled trail and cross the desert south of Great Salt Lake. He said it would save three hundred miles.

Ninety emigrants, including the Reeds, took his advice. Saving miles cost a month of precious travel time, and the Reeds lost the rest of their oxen. The Pioneer Palace Car, left behind, looked like a monument in the desert sands.

At the Humboldt River a young teamster attacked Virginia's father. Reed stabbed his assailant to death. It was clearly self defense, but the other emigrants, resenting Reed's prosperity, banished him from the train. Reed was not even allowed a gun for hunting or self defense against Indians.

It was October, and the emigrants now worried about deep snow in the Sierras. They suggested that Reed redeem himself by traveling on alone to Sutter's Fort and bringing back help for the mountain crossing. Virginia sneaked away from the train to take her father a rifle and ammunition, and hen rode on alone into the cold, bare desert.

By now the Reeds were down to two mules. Virginia cried all day when they left Billy behind. Mrs. Reed and one child rode one mule and Virginia and the other two children rode the other. Before they reached the Truckee River, both mules had perished, and the Reeds were all afoot.

The emigrants struggled into the Sierras through waist-deep snow. They reached a lake near the summit and could go no further. They butchered their few remaining oxen and stored the meat in the snow. The

Reeds and another family shared a crude shelter, covered with an ox-hide roof. The women cooked and re-cooked ox-bones. Mrs. Reed had hidden away a few apples, some beans, and a tiny piece of bacon. When she sat down with her children at Christmas, she said: "Eat slowly, children. There is plenty for all."

Virginia and her mother trapped field mice for food. They killed their five family dogs and ate them. For seven weeks they ate nothing but boiled strips of ox-hide, cut away from their roof. By then the ox meat, horns, and hooves had all been eaten. The Reed family was the only one that did not eat human flesh in that winter tragedy.

Virginia, her mother, and two others tried to cross the mountain. They were too weak. After five days they returned, defeated. Virginia's feet were severely frostbitten.

The Patrick Breen family lived for a time in the same shelter as the Reeds. Breen, an Irish Catholic, prayed often and earnestly. Some days he prayed almost continuously. Virginia, impressed with Breen's praying, promised God she would become a Catholic if rescued.

On February 19 a rescue party from Sutter's Fort arrived. Virginia, her mother, and one brother were strong enough to travel. On their way over the mountains, they met Virginia's father, coming with another rescue party.

Three months after Virginia escaped from the mountains, her weight was up to eighty pounds. She kept her promise and became a Catholic.

Her love of horses continued. The letter to her cousin was filled with descriptions of California vaqueros, their horses, equipment, and skills. Virginia became one of California's champion women riders. She grew up a beauty and married John Murphy, a young army officer. They had nine children.

Virginia's letter to her cousin, describing the journey, ended with some good advice: "Dont let this letter disharten anybody. Never take no cutofs and hury along as fast as you can."

Suggested reading: Virginia Murphy, "Across the Plains in the Donner Party (1846)" in *The Century Magazine, 42* (1891).

TWO FAMILIES IN THE SIERRAS

Sometimes the small children in the George Donner and Jacob Donner families found it hard to understand how they were related. George had two girls, Elitha, 14, and Leanna, 12, from his second marriage. He and Tamsen, his third wife, had three more girls, Frances, 6, Georgia, 4, and Eliza, 3. The seven children of Jacob and Elizabeth Donner also divided into two parts. They had five children together, George, 9, Mary, 7, Isaac, 5, Samuel, 4, and Lewis, 3. Solomon Hook, 14, and William, his 12-year-old brother, were Elizabeth's boys from a prior marriage. Both families were close, Tamsen a good mother for George's older daughters, and Jacob a good father for Elizabeth's older sons.

George and Jacob were brothers. The fact that George Donner's second wife (Elitha's and Leanna's mother) was Elizabeth's sister complicated the relationships. It made Jacob's "Donner" children first cousins of George and Tamsen's three little girls and double cousins of the two older girls. The Hook boys were first cousins of George's older girls (their mothers were sisters), but unrelated by blood to George's and Tamsen's three little girls.

The children of both families shared a horrible tragedy in the California Sierras in the terrible winter of 1846-47. The George Donner daughters all escaped, but one Hook boy and three of Jacob's and Elizabeth's children perished, as did all four of the parents.

After many delays and four deaths on the trail, the emigrants reached Truckee Lake, just below the Sierra crest, in late October. Elitha and Leanna from the George Donner family, and George, Jr. and William Hook from the Jacob Donner family all left with the first rescue party on February 23. William died from over-eating when he reached food. The other three survived.

Elizabeth was strong enough to go with the same rescue party, but she chose to stay with her younger children. Samuel and Lewis were too small to walk in the deep snow, and the adults in the party had already been assigned all the children they could carry. Solomon stayed to help his mother. The rescuers also asked Tamsen to go with them. But George had injured himself, and she stayed with him and their younger daughters.

Jacob Donner had died back in December. He told Elizabeth that he wanted her to use his body for food to keep her and the children alive. Elizabeth said she would die before using it herself, but she did eventually cook and serve to her children her husband's heart and liver and the sparse, stringy flesh she could strip from his bones.

Mary and Isaac Donner and Solomon Hook left with the second rescue party on March 3. Three days later, after their party had traveled about a dozen miles, the worst storm of the winter raged through the mountains. Isaac Donner died during the storm. The three adults in the group and the children in their families told the rescue party leaders they would rather die in the pit they had dug in the snow for shelter than continue. Mary Donner wanted to go on, but she had burned her frozen feet in the fire while asleep. She tried to walk, but the leaders had to carry her back and leave her in the snow pit, too.

Solomon Hook survived. So did Mary, but only after a later rescue party returned for her. By then, one adult and another child had died in the snow pit. All the survivors there had eaten human flesh, scraped from the bones of the dead.

Back at the starvation camp, Lewis Donner died during the same 3-day storm that killed his brother Isaac. Their mother, Elizabeth, died shortly after. When Tamsen found Samuel alone at the Jacob Donner tent, she took him home and put him in bed with his uncle George.

A third rescue party reached the survivors on March 13. They left immediately with four children, including Tamsen's three daughters. They asked Tamsen to go with them. She was strong enough, but she refused to leave her husband. The three girls all survived.

A month passed before anyone returned to the lake. By then, George Donner, Tamsen, and little Samuel were all dead.

All five of George Donner's daughters married and lived to old ages. Leanna was almost one hundred when she died. Mary Donner married Congressman S. O. Houghton in 1859. She died in childbirth the next year.

The complicated relationships in the Donner families continued. After Mary Donner Houghton died, Congressman Houghton married Mary's double cousin, Eliza.

Suggested reading: C. F. McGlashan, *History of the Donner Party* (Stanford: Stanford University Press, 1947).

A WALK IN THE WOODS

Nine-year-old Arenia Thankful Lewis and her brothers, eleven-year-old Jimmy and six-year-old Johnny, were walking home from school in July, 1863. As they often did, the children broke up their three-mile hike through the Butte County, California, foothills that day by stopping at their grandmother's for a cool drink of water.

"You children go on along now," grandmother said after she put the dipper back. "Your folks will be expecting you."

"Yes, ma'am," they chorused.

As they walked along Littlefield Creek, a sudden rifle shot startled Arenia, and she was horrified to see Jimmy pitch into the water, blood pouring out of his back. Four Indians jumped out from behind a cluster of grape vines and began throwing rocks at the dying boy. Arenia and little Johnny trembled with fear as they watched the gruesome slaughter of their brother.

Six more Indians joined the attackers. One grabbed the hat from their crushed, bloody victim and clapped it gleefully on his own head. Two others grabbed Arenia and Johnny by the arms and jerked them along the trail, as they set out toward the mountains.

When Arenia realized that some of their captors could speak English, she pleaded with them.

"Please let us go," she begged. "I can see our house from here — just down there in the valley." She pointed with a shaking hand. "Our pa and ma will be expecting us. Johnny, here, is only six, you know."

"No we going to take you OUR home. Your home no more."

"You father follow?" asked another Indian.

"He sure will." Arenia tried to sound brave.

"We better be moving on."

The Indians banged their rifle butts against their captives' ribs to hurry them along.

"Sister, they are hurting me," Johnny wailed, tears rolling down his pallid face.

By dark the barefooted children were shedding blood as well as tears. The Indians kept prodding them to keep them moving.

In the moonlight, Arenia could see a family friend, John Leonard, driving nearby in a wagon. The Indians rushed into some thick brush, threw the children down, and almost smothered them to keep them from calling for help.

Later, crossing a dusty road, they carried Johnny and beat Arenia with a rifle to make her walk tiptoe so as to not leave recognizable tracks. Arenia could hear barking from the dog of Mister Nance, another neighbor she knew.

Later in the night, Johnny could no longer keep up, no matter how much they beat him. Four Indians carried him off the trail into the brush.

"Goodbye, sister," Johnny said, his face drawn and tears rolling down his cheeks. He knew what would come.

"Goodbye," was all Arenia could say.

She heard noises as though rocks were crashing through brush, and she assumed little Johnny was being stoned to death like their older brother. She did summon the strength to ask the Indians if she could go back and kiss her brother. They refused.

"No," one said. "We must reach camp. When we get there, we put sticks around you and burn you up while we dance."

Some of them laughed at the girl. Others ripped the skirt of Arenia's dress into tatters and set fire to it. They laughed as the terrified girl frantically beat the flames out with her hands.

Arenia heard a rooster crow and she begged again for her freedom. The sky in the east was getting lighter.

The Indians swung their rifles at her to keep her moving.

After they crossed Little Chico Creek, the Indians killed a steer and butchered it. As they rested, Arenia noticed that one Indian had a lame leg.

If I act friendly and quit begging, they might be put off guard, the nine-year-old girl thought.

"How did you hurt your leg?" she asked.

"A white man shot me."

Arenia could think of nothing more to say.

The Indians washed the steer's blood off their bodies in the creek. Then they distributed the meat among them and moved on.

Arenia was so tired now she could hardly move. She was also discouraged. She didn't know how long it would take to reach the Indians' camp, and she expected to be killed once they got there. She was so exhausted she lagged behind, without even thinking any more about trying to escape.

They were moving along the edge of a ravine. Arenia dropped down on a large rock and turned to the one Indian in the rear.

"Please let me rest on this rock and I'll catch up with you," she said.

The Indian carried two guns in addition to his share of the steer meat. He pointed one gun at Arenia.

"If you try to get away, I'll kill you."

As soon as the Indian disappeared into the brush ahead, Arenia rolled over and over, down into the deep ravine.

When she got to her feet, she ran over a mile to another crossing on Big Chico Creek. The barefoot girl now ran through thistles, thinking it would keep her from leaving tracks.

She heard the Indians coming after her, and she hid under some driftwood in the creek. She trembled when they got a hundred yards from her, but they did not see her. The water was deep, and she almost drowned getting across after the Indians moved away.

"I would rather have drowned than have them take me again," she would say later.

Arenia ran over a mile and reached the Thomasson place.

"Oh, child," Mrs. Thomasson said, "where have you come from."

Mrs. Thomasson washed and greased Arenia's bloody feet and picked out the stickers and briers.

The news of Arenia's escape spread, and soon her parents found her.

Arenia went with the posse to search for the Indians. She showed them where the beef had been butchered and she found the rock which she had rolled from to start her escape. She showed them where Johnny had been left. The posse found his body. He, like his brother, had been beaten to death with rocks.

They only found one Indian. They captured him and tied him to a tree. Arenia's father and other men shot him over and over again.

Nothing was said about whether Arenia recognized him as one of her captors. It would have made no difference to the California settlers, many of them with children of their own.

Suggested reading: George C. Mansfield, *History of Butte County, California* (Los Angeles: Historic Record Co., 1918).

ANGELIC DREAM

On February 19, 1847, rescuers reached the Donner-Reed emigrant party, stranded for four months in deep Sierra snow. Four days later twenty-three of the survivors started over the pass. The others, too weak to travel, stayed behind. Margaret Reed and her four children were among those selected to leave. Her husband, James Reed, had been banished from the emigrant group earlier and sent on ahead to Sutter's Fort. Hopefully he would be coming back to bring help.

Eight-year-old Patty Reed and her three-year-old brother, Tommy, could not keep up. The adults and older children could follow in the footsteps of those ahead, but Patty and Tommy had to struggle over a ridge of snow between each step and the next. After two miles Tommy could go no further. With seventeen children in the group, no adults were available to carry him. Patty was also exhausted.

"They'll have to go back, Mrs. Reed," the men said. "We're sorry, but they'll never be able to keep up."

Margaret Reed was frantic, knowing that her family had to be divided. Should she go on, hoping to escape starvation and find her husband, somewhere on ahead? Or should she go back with Patty and the baby, knowing that at least Virginia and James might possibly see their father again?

Aquilla Glover, the rescue leader, was a member of the Masons, like Margaret's husband. She agreed to stay with the group and her older children when Glover promised on his honor as a Mason that he would go back for Patty and Tommy as soon as he had taken this group to safety.

As the men carried Patty and her little brother back down to the lake, Patty solemnly told them how she felt.

"I don't mind going back to look after Tommy," she said, nodding her head gravely. "But I know I'll never again see the rest of my family."

The men choked back their tears.

Five days later the Glover group met James Reed coming up with another rescue party. After a tearful reunion with his wife and his two older children, James pushed on, reaching the camp by the lake on March 1. He saw Patty sitting on the roof of a shelter, her feet on the snow. When she recognized her father, she clapped her hands joyfully and tried to run to him, but she was too weak. James lifted her tenderly out of the snow. After an emotional embrace, he asked about the baby. Patty led him inside the shelter, where Tommy lay in bed.

Tommy now considered Patty his new mother. Not until she assured him that the stranger was really his father, would Tommy smile.

On March 3 Reed and his three companions started out with seventeen refugees. It took three days to cross the pass, about five miles away. Then a three-day, hurricane-force storm hit, and no one could move. During the storm little Isaac Donner died as he slept between his sister and Patty Reed.

When the storm ended, the Breen and the Graves families said they would rather die in the snow than struggle on. The four rescuers and three children — Patty, her baby brother, and Solomon Hook, Isaac Donner's half brother, — kept going. Patty, the weakest, refused to let her father carry her.

Later that day Patty cried out with joy that angels and brilliant stars were all around her. Her shrunken face broke into radiant smiles as she whispered about the things she saw, beautiful beyond description. The men realized that Patty lay at the doorway of death. They stopped and wrapped her chilled body in a blanket, rubbing her little arms and legs briskly.

The total supply of food for the whole party were some crumbs that Reed carried in the thumb of his woolen mitten. He put the crumbs in his mouth to warm and moisten them. He gently pressed them into his daughter's mouth. The girl revived and felt sad as the beautiful lights and angels disappeared from her view.

Although Patty still hovered close to death, it was light enough to travel, and the men wanted to reach a cache of food they had left on the way up. They struggled on in the deep snow, talking about how the courage and faith of an eight-year-old girl had inspired them. One of them, famous even among western bullwhackers for his expressive vocabulary, said — between expletives — that she was an angel on earth.

When the party camped that evening, Patty pulled from her bosom a tiny wooden doll. No one knew that she had kept it there during the long months of starvation. Patty sat and held the doll, as the men looked on in silence. She carefully told the doll all about the events of the last few days. She repeated over and over the joy she felt when she dreamed about the angels and the stars.

Patty Reed married Frank Lewis in Santa Cruz on Christmas day in 1856. She and Frank had eight children. She lived to ninety-three. She always remembered her dream about angels as the nicest experience she ever had.

Suggested reading: George R. Stewart, *Ordeal by Hunger* (Boston: Houghton Mifflin Company, 1960).

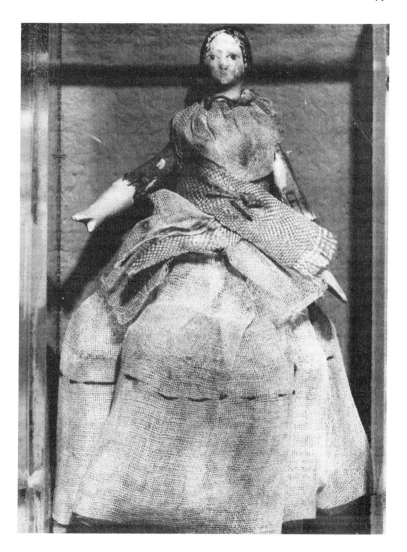

PATTY REED'S DOLL

Nevada Historical Society

BILLY LAMBKIN'S CHRISTMAS SEASON

The boy's pitiful cries stopped J. Goldsborough Bruff as he carried firewood to his northern Sierra trail camp on a cold November 16, 1849. Bruff saw the small boy lying on damp blankets, trying to pull up a wet buffalo robe that was too heavy for his feeble attempts.

"What's your name son?" Bruff asked.

"Billy Lambkin."

"Where's your pa?"

"I — I don't know." The boy spoke with a slight lisp and was close to tears.

Bruff gathered wood and started a fire. Then he pulled the robe over Billy, making the boy as comfortable as possible.

"You be quiet now, and I'll see if I can find your pa and send him back to you with something to eat."

Billy nodded and smiled weakly, bewildered at this care-giving stranger.

Inquiring around, Bruff learned that Billy was just four years old. His father, "an inhuman wretch," had left the boy's mother, "a reputable wife," in St. Louis to start for California with another woman who was pregnant. That woman had her baby on the trail and it died at four months. The woman died later, back on the Humboldt River.

Two other men in the camp were traveling with the boy's father, and one was familiar with the man's reputation back in St. Louis. He told Bruff that Lambkin had taken his small son with him solely to spite his wife.

Bruff found Lambkin laughing and talking at one of the many camp fires spread along the Lassen Trail, near present Lassen National Park. He told the man his little boy was crying.

"Yes, damn him," Lambkin snorted, "let him cry. Hell, the kid's always crying."

After a few rough words, Bruff stalked away. He did tell Lambkin that if he had the means, he would protect the boy himself.

Bruff was one of eighteen children, only five of whom reached maturity. He and a few men were guarding their group's equipment and supplies while the rest went ahead to the Sacramento River for food and mules so they could all move on down to the goldfields. Bruff had been getting by largely by hunting.

The next day Bruff baked some mildewed grain into a cake and gave small bits to Billy from time to time.

"This is all I got, sonny," he said. "Hunting hasn't been too good."

On November 20, Bruff exchanged bitter words with Lambkin about his treatment of his son. During the argument, Bruff reached for his pistol, hanging from his belt, but Lambkin ran before Bruff could pull it out of the holster.

Two days later, Bruff caught Lambkin prowling around his camp and drove him off. Bruff wrote in his diary, "The hope of his doing something for his child prevents me from treating him as he deserves."

Later that day, Bruff gave the boy a spool of cotton to play with. As Billy unwound it he kept saying mournfully, "Mother's cotton, Mother's scissors, Mother has bread, Mother has cake."

Bruff wrote in his dairy, "My compassion may prolong your sufferings, son, but I cannot alleviate them much."

The next day Billy cried constantly for bread. Bruff had collected a half peck of acorns, but unfortunately they weren't the right kind to grind for meal.

Lambkin was not seen for the next week or so, and Bruff looked out for the boy as best he could. He heard that a woman in the camp might be willing to care for Billy, but nothing came of it.

Bruff next mentions Billy in his diary for December 15, after another unsuccessful hunt. "The poor little child is failing," Bruff wrote. "He is pale and weak, with sunken eyes, for want of bread and proper food. We shorten our rations in order to sustain him as long as possible. We go to bed often very hungry, when the child has a piece of meat laying by him, after eating hearty. He does not suffer from cold, except occasionally complaining of his toes.

The next day Billy was bleeding from his nose and ears. The snow was very deep, and Bruff and his partner took Billy into their wagon with them, where he slept at their feet. Bruff was suffering from fever, and he thought his eyesight might be affected. They had hunted that day for carcasses of dead oxen, buried in the snow.

By December 21 Billy was crying most of the nights. Bruff decided that if they could not find an ox carcass, they would have to kill their little puppy for one more meal.

They did find an ox the next day under a hump in the snow. "The boy ate like a young wolf," Bruff wrote.

They were surprised the meat did not taste bad. Now that they had a food larder they had to protect it from wolves and bears.

By Christmas day Bruff and his partner had found another ox carcass in the snow, and they scraped off some meat. They boiled it in a kettle, adding a squirrel and three deer-leg bones. After a hearty dinner, Billy watched and listened as the two men smoked their pipes, sang songs, and wondered how their friends back home were enjoying themselves on the holiday.

Around a lively fire made from cutting up the running gear of abandoned wagons, Bruff and his partner spoke of roast sirloin, mince-pies, eggnog, and plum pudding. Bruff wrote that Billy was doing well, and he thought they could now keep the puppy.

Bruff remembered how he had shuddered at home while reading accounts of the voraciousness of Russian soldiers eating train oil and tallow candles. He wrote that he would feel fortunate to have such rations now. In fact, they had already fried several candles with their meat.

Billy suffered from lack of exercise. Bruff wrote about the little boy's ability to deceive his protectors. "The poor little fellow had been so brutally treated by his father — and probably with a tincture of his father's composition — that he is exceedingly stubborn and artful. While we were present, he would feign perfect inability to stand or walk; and, as previously mentioned, I have been compelled to take him under the arms, and run him across the lodge chamber for exercise, when persuasion, threats, etc. were unavailing to induce him to stand.

"Yet finding things on the floor that we knew were out of his reach when we went out, we watched to ascertain if he possibly could move about; and judge our astonishment, one day, to see him climb up in a chair (we had several old rush bottom chairs found in an abandoned wagon), AND get something down from a hanging shelf. When he heard us he ran quite sprightly and seated himself by the fire!

"His abode, in the wagon, is the most comfortable one here; several blankets and coverlids under, and several others to cover him, and these aired and changed as often as we can. We give him plenty of meat — more than he can consume — and coffee and water. And I frequently look in to see that he is as comfortable as circumstances permit."

By December 29, Bruff had lived for forty-seven days on bad beef and venison, eight on putrid smoked beef, and eight on the ancient ox meat found under the snow. The next day two men returned from a trip to the settlements. They brought flour, and Bruff allocated a half pound to flour cakes for Billy. They all ate like hungry wolves. After supper Billy seemed unusually still, except when he had a convulsion. Bruff decided to see if they could get to the settlements while Billy still had a chance to survive.

About three p. m. on New Year's Eve, pulling a hastily-built sled, Bruff and two men started for the settlements. They had piled their tent, bedding, utensils, and guns on the sled. Billy, wrapped in a blanket, was carefully laid on top of the load. About seven that evening they staggered into a shelter occupied by other stranded travelers. Bruff collapsed at the entrance.

Bruff's two companions continued on at midnight, hoping to be back from the settlements in four days with food. They left four bread rolls with Bruff. He divided them evenly with Billy.

Bruff tried to feed a little broth to Billy the next morning, New Year's Day. But by eleven o'clock, Billy was "extricated from all the hardships of this life."

Bruff washed the boy's body in the snow and wrapped it in a piece of white cotton. He buried Billy the next day with this inscription on a head board:

WILLIAM
infant son of
LAMBKIN
an
Unnatural
Father
Died Jan 1
1850

Four months later, Bruff was on his way back to Washington to resume his government employment as a draftsman. He had decided that mining was not for him. He stopped by Billy's grave on the way up the trail.

The grave had been dug up, probably by someone who thought supplies had been cached there. Bruff found the skull about fifty yards down the hill. He picked it up with a stick, returned it to the grave, and filled the grave in again. He had never heard anything more about Billy's unnatural father.

Suggested reading: Georgia W. Read (ed.) *Gold Rush, The Journals, Drawings, and other papers of J. Goldsborough Bruff*, (New York: Columbia University Press, 1949).

ORDEAL AT OKOBOJI

On March 8, 1857, the Gardner family rose before dawn. With an early start on his eighty-mile trip to Fort Dodge for provisions, Rowland Gardner could reach the cabin of another settler for his first night on the trail. The summer before, he and a few others had settled around the Okoboji Lakes and Spirit Lake of northwestern Iowa. The local Winnebagoes were friendly, but not the Sioux.

Thirteen-year-old Abigail and younger brother, Rowland, Junior, were up with their parents to eat breakfast. Also living in the cabin were an older married sister, Mary, her husband, Harvey Luce, and their little boy and baby girl.

An Indian walked in as the two families were sitting down to eat. They made a place for him at the table, and invited him to share their frugal meal. Before the meal ended, renegade Sioux chief, Inkpaduta, and thirteen more warriors, along with some of their women and children, had crowded in to share the nervous hospitality.

After the meager stores in the cabin had been distributed, the Indians turned insolent, demanding ammunition and guns. One would have shot Harvey Luce had Harvey not seized a gun first and pointed it at the Indian.

Not until late forenoon were all the Indians out of the cabin. But then they started shooting the cattle, and Gardner sent his son-in-law to warn neighbors. Gardner said he would stay to protect the rest of the family.

Abigail's sister threw her arms around Harvey and sobbed that she would never see him again. About two hours after Harvey left, the frightened family heard more gunfire. Gardner left to investigate, but returned immediately, saying nine Indians were approaching.

"I've got two guns," he said. "I'll kill some while they're killing us."

"Oh, don't, Rowland," his wife pleaded. "If we have to die, let us do it innocent of shedding blood ourselves."

The Indians were allowed in. They demanded flour, and, as Gardner turned to get it, they shot him through the heart. Mrs. Gardner and Mary grabbed for a gun, but the Indians clubbed them. Then they dragged the two women outside and killed them in what Abigail called "a shocking and cruel manner."

Abigail cringed in a chair with her sister's baby in her arms, her six-year-old brother on one side and her four-year-old nephew on the other, both clinging to her in terror. They watched, helpless, as the Indians ransacked the house.

Finally, the raiders tore the three small children away from Abigail, took them outside, and beat them to death with pieces of stovewood. Abigail would never forget the piteous cries for protection which she could no longer provide.

Abigail begged the Indians to kill her, too, but they continued with their orgy of destruction. Finally, when they were through killing and scalping, they dragged Abigail outside, and she realized they would keep her as a captive. All of her family had been killed except her sixteen-year-old sister, Eliza, who was caring for a sick neighbor.

After a mile of travel, Abigail's captors reached a group of burning cabins, where the unearthly war-whoops of other Indians mingled with the screams of two settlers, burning to death inside. Abigail recognized many of the bodies scattered on the forest floor.

Abigail counted about twenty bodies in the first day's slaughter. After a frenzied scalp dance among their victims, the Indians, exhausted, fell asleep. Terror-stricken after the Indians' hideous revelry, Abigail gave no thought to attempting escape.

The slaughter continued the next day as the warriors, now painted black for war, attacked the settlers at East Okoboji Lake and Spirit Lake. On this day the Indians killed all the men and children — some by smashing heads against trees — and all the women but Lydia Noble and Mrs. Thatcher, who were taken captive.

That evening the three captives were told by signs and gestures to braid their hair and paint their faces like Indian women.

Abigail was plunged ito a hopeless despair after seeing the "inhuman monsters" murder so many whom she had loved. She longed for her own death, and whenever an Indian threatened torture to compel her obedience, she would bow her head and wait silently. Then she realized that her tearless acquiescence and willingness to die filled them with admiration. They mistook it for great bravery, which they admired but did not think white women possessed.

The Indians found one more settler's cabin, killed the man and took the wife, Margaret Marble, captive.

After traveling northwest for six weeks, the Indians reached the Big Sioux River near present Flandreau, South Dakota. There, Abigail and Mrs. Thatcher walked out on a downed tree which bridged the flooded stream. Some Indian boys pushed Mrs. Thatcher into the river. The woman fought the icy current and struggled back to the bank to clutch a tree root. Other Indians used poles to shove her back into the stream. Still more Indians joined the sport, throwing rocks and clubs at the nineteen-year old woman. Finally an Indian shot her and she disappeared under the icy, roiling waters.

The remaining captives were deeply affected by the wanton murder. Lydia Noble took it the hardest as she was a cousin by marriage of the victim. She tried to persuade Abigail to go with her to the river and drown themselves. The young girl, who earlier had pleaded with the Indians to kill her, thought suicide was not Christian, and she refused.

On May 6, while they were camped near a small lake about thirty miles west of the Big Sioux River, two Sioux Indians from a reservation in Minnesota visited Inkpaduta's band. They wanted to buy Abigail but were informed she was not for sale. Instead they bought Margaret Marble, and took her away.

Abigail did not grieve for Margaret Marble as she had for Mrs. Thatcher, as she assumed the woman had bettered her condition by being with Indians who were willing to buy her. Abgail wrote: "I was certain she could not fall into worse hands than those from which she had escaped."

By now Abigail and Lydia Noble and their captors were far west of the Big Sioux River, farther, she thought, than any white person had been before. The stolen provisions had been exhausted, and the Indians and captives lived on wild game and roots. Birds were prepared for the kettle by pulling off only the roughest feathers — no washing or cleaning. Beaver and otter were singed to loosen the thickest fur and then pitched into the boiling pot.

About four weeks after Margaret Marble was bought and carried away, Abigail and Lydia were sold to a man in a small party of Yankton Sioux. Abigail did not know what he paid, but she knew he expected to make a profit by selling them to whites.

But Lydia refused the order of Inkpaduta's son, Roaring Cloud, to come out of their lodge. He beat Lydia to death in front of Abigail, who could never forget the woman's dying moans. Abigail was forced to watch the Indians use Lydia's body for target practice. Then they drew their knives and carved the corpse into pieces.

Now Abigail was alone with the inhuman murderers — no one to talk to, no one to mourn with her. Every night she prayed that God would take her life. One Indian had cut off Lydia's long braids, tied them to a stick, and repeatedly struck Abigail in the face with his newly-made toy.

Abigail had been keeping track of the days so she would know when it was Sunday. Now, she lost track of time. The days had turned warm, and new leaves appeared on the trees, and bright grass and fowers blossomed on the prairie. But a despondent Abigail saw no beauty, only ugliness and despair.

A few days after the murder of Lydia Noble, the Indians reached a large band of Yankton Sioux on the James River. Abigail counted almost two hundred lodges — two thousand persons. She was apparently the first white person these people had ever seen. They entered her lodge at all hours to examine her and comment on her hair, eyes, and complexion.

Abigail had given up all hope of rescue. Only one horse — a doctor's pony — of the seventeen stolen was still alive. The rest had died of neglect or cruelty and had been eaten. Abigail assumed Margaret Marble was dead, as she knew Mrs. Thatcher and Julia Noble were. She and the one horse were all that were left from the long ago raid.

But on May 30, three Indians came to her lodge dressed in coats and white shirts. She knew they must be close, again, to the borders of the civilized world. She wanted to communicate but dared not.

The new Indians said nothing, but councils began. They went on for three days. During that time, Inkpaduta's people and the Yanktons amused themselves by telling Abigail she would be taken a long way off and then killed. One said she would be drowned, another that she would be beaten to death, another that she would be tied to a stake and burned alive, another that she would slowly be carved into pieces.

But a Yankton woman told the despondent girl the stories were false, and that Abigail was being bought by Indians who would sell her back to the whites. Did the girl dare hope?

The Yankton woman had told the truth. The price was paid — two horses, twelve blankets, two kegs of gunpowder, twenty pounds of tobacco, and calico, ribbons and small articles. Then Abigail's new owners — intelligent, middle-aged men, prominent in the mission church — started toward St. Paul.

After nine days of travel, they came to an area where Indians and half-bloods lived in cabins. There Abigail learned that her purchasers were acting under instructions of the United States Indian agent. Hope began to rise. She also learned that Margaret Marble had gone on to St. Paul about a month before.

Abigail had been painted and her hair heavily oiled for most of her capture. Now she worked hard every day to wash off the paint and oil so she would be presentable to people like herself.

They reached St. Paul on June 22. Thanks be to God, her three and one half month ordeal had finally ended! The thirteen-year-old girl was soon re-united with her sister, Eliza, who was now married.

On August 16, still a girl by age but an old woman by experience, Abigail married William Wilson, a cousin of both Julia Noble and Mrs. Thatcher. Abigail named her first child Albert for her sister's Albert, who had been torn from her arms on the day of the massacre.

Abigail never recovered from the injuries she received during her capture. She was an invalid for most of the rest of her life.

Suggested reading: Abigail Gardner Sharp, *History of the Spirit Lake Massacre* (Des Moines: Wallace-Homestead Book. Co, 1971).

MINNESOTA CAPTIVES

The Gottfried Buce family were among the German immigrants who settled in the Minnesota River Valley in 1860. Buce and his wife, Wilhelmina, had immigrated from Germany to Wisconsin two years before. Now, they and their four children moved further west, looking for better land and opportunities. August was the oldest, with little sisters, five-year-old Wilhelmina, usually called Minnie, two-year-old Amelia, and baby Augusta. Caroline was born on the journey west.

The Buce children had no school, but their parents taught them to read German, and the following spring arrangements were made for a German minister to preach once a month. The children learned a little English in Sunday school, but they learned more Sioux from the Santees who visited almost every day.

The Santees seemed friendly, but one day the family discovered one of their calves had been killed with a hind quarter removed and the rest left to rot. Buce brought the calf in and saved what meat he could. He remarked sarcastically that it was nice of the Indians to leave them some of his own calf.

The next morning fifty mounted Indians, all painted for war, rode up to the Buce cabin, and Buce sat at his table unable to move. His wife went to see what the visitors wanted and came back in, laughing.

"They say it was a Chippewa that killed the little calf," she said. "They tracked him to our house, and want to help us find him."

Buce went with the Santees until they reached the place the calf was killed, but then he returned home. "They're so determined the Chippewa to kill, that home I came right back," he said. "Better I lose a dozen calves than one Indian should another kill."

The Santees returned that afternoon with the Chippewa. Delighted at capturing him alive so they could torture him to death, they wanted Buce to come to the killing and the feast to follow. He refused.

Spring 1862 brought many new settlers. The churchgoers divided into two divisions, and each one had services twice a month. The settlers noticed that the attitudes of the Santees seemed to change. They became disagreeable and ill-natured. They seldom visited any more. When they passed the settlers, they were cold and sullen, often refusing to speak.

Early that summer, Buce, now thirty-three, found Indians camped in the woods where they had cut down all his young timber. He told them they could cut all the lodge poles they needed for their actual use, but should leave the rest of the trees. An Indian woman grabbed a butcher knife and chased him away. When Buce told this to his wife, she laughed at him for allowing an old squaw to drive him out of his own woods.

In early August chiefs at the agency, pleading for long-promised government food, were told by trader Andrew Myrick, "If you're hungry you can all eat grass for all I care."

Sunday, August 17, seemed peaceful when church services were held at the Letton cabin, a mile and a half from the Buce place. At Sunday school Mr. Mannweiler, the district superintendent, gave each child a little blue card containing a bible verse to memorize. Those who succeeded would get a pretty red card at the next worship service.

Over a hundred adults and thirty children came to church that day. The next day three-fourths of them would be killed by Santees under Chief Little Crow. With five hundred settlers burned alive, tortured, or hacked to pieces, it would be one of the most savage Indian uprisings in North American history.

That Monday, Buce was making hay about a mile east of their cabin when his wife heard gunfire in the woods. She assumed it was Indians firing at a mark. She needed sewing needles, and she sent August to the neighboring Rosler cabin to borrow some. He returned to say the Roslers were all asleep. "Mrs. Rosler and the little boy were lying on the floor," he said, "the boy's ear had blood running out. The big boy was lying in their clay pit, all covered with clay."

"Dear God," Mrs. Buce moaned. "The Indians have killed them. We must fly for our lives."

She told the children to stay in the cabin while she ran for their father. But August and Minnie refused to stay. "Then take the little ones and meet us in the south corn field," the frantic woman replied. "Father and I will meet you there."

August carried baby Bertha, Minnie carried little Caroline, and five-year-old Augusta and four-year-old Amelia ran with them. The children had just reached the field when whooping Indians ran from the direction of the neighboring John Boelter cabin and rushed their house. The children reached the south side of the field, where their parents were waiting.

Minnie thought they would have been safe in the field, but her father took the baby from August and started across the open prairie. Her mother took Caroline from Minnie and ran to stop him, but it was useless.

The Indians, having trashed the Buce home, ran outside to return to Boelter's, and they saw Mr. Buce carrying the baby. Soon twenty Indian men and a few women set upon the family. Mr. Buce pleaded with the Indians to take all his property but to let him and his family go. One Indian leveled a double-barreled shotgun, fired both barrels, and Buce and his baby fell dead. By this time, Mrs. Buce was sitting on a rock with little Caroline in her lap. The same Indian that had killed Buce and the baby calmly reloaded his gun and killed the mother and Caroline. Minnie wrote that she could hear Caroline's scream for many years.

Minnie saw the Indian reloading his gun and looking at her and Amelia as though they were next. She jumped up and ran, accidentally coming to where her father lay dead. The next thing she remembered was an Indian holding her in his arms, peering intently into her face. She screamed, and he put her down.

August then told her to not be afraid, as he thought the Indians intended to take them captive and not kill them. Minnie looked around quickly. "Where's Augusta?" she demanded. "I don't see Augusta!"

The three children looked for their sister. An Indian said, "nepo." Minnie knew the word meant "killed" or "dead" but she insisted on seeing the girl. An Indian took her by the hand and led her, August and Amelia following, to where their sister lay on the ground, face downward. They could see no blood on the girl, so Minnie, hoping she might be alive, turned the body over. When Minnie "looked upon the little face, once so sweet and rosy, but now so pallid and ghastly in the blaze of the hot August sun," she knew the truth and was ready to go with the Indians.

Their captors took the children past the Boelter's. Minnie saw the bodies of three of the Boelter children. Grandma Boelter's body lay inside the cabin, hacked apart at every joint. Minnie dreamed and cried in her sleep about that all winter. She thought Grandma Boelter was such a nice old lady.

Justina Boelter, who had just lost her husband and three children, escaped with two other children and hid in the woods for nine weeks before some soldiers found them. By then one of the surviving children had starved to death. Justina later married her brother-in-law, who had lost his wife and three daughters in the August 18 attack.

Minnie, seven, was taken into the home of an old Indian with two wives. Minnie recognized the old man as the killer of her parents. The Indian family had much of the stolen Buce property.

When Minnie saw the younger wife wearing her mother's dress, she fell to the ground sobbing. The woman never wore the dress again in Minnie's presence.

The Indians moved southwest, and Minnie saw other neighbors from time to time who had been captured. She also recognized Indians who had visited their cabin before the outbreak. The Indians told her they had cut her brother's throat because he had cried, but Minnie saw August from time to time. The Indians had also told August that Minnie had been killed for trying to run away.

Minnie once recognized the body of their little dog as the Indians were preparing a huge dog feast. She resolved to not eat that meal, but it was a religious celebration, and women and children were not allowed, anyway.

On September 19 Minnie heard the cannon fire at the Battle of Wood Lake, where Colonel Henry Sibley and fifteen hundred militia defeated Little Crow and his Sioux. A few days later a young Indian woman took Minnie and Amelia to a hill, near present Montevideo, where white captives were being herded into a circle with a white flag flying overhead. Minnie thought they were planning to kill the prisoners, and she refused to go. Two Indian girls carried her in. She saw August, and he told her that the soldiers had defeated the Indians and they would soon be free.

A few days later the Indians surrendered their prisoners, about a hundred white women and children. The next few days, as the captives were brought in to Fort Ridgley, were emotional ones. Some settlers learned that children and relatives they thought dead were really alive. Others, of course, learned the opposite. Minnie and her sister were taken into the home of Rev. and Mrs. Frederic Emde. Brother August was taken by a minister in St. Paul.

Fifteen hundred Santees, captured at Wood Lake, were tried by a five-man military commission, and three hundred seven sentenced to death. While the condemned Indians were still in the army's custody, enraged civilians, some still re-burying their dead, attacked. The soldiers fixed bayonets and drove the whites back to protect their prisoners.

When President Lincoln learned that the average hearing by the military commission had taken ten minutes, he reviewed the records and pardoned all but thirty-eight Indians. These were hanged at Mankato on December 28, the largest public execution in the nation's history.

Trader Myrick had been killed on August 18. When his body was found a few days later, the mouth was stuffed full of grass.

Minnie eventually married and settled not many miles from her old cabin in the Minnesota River bottom lands. She vowed to never look at it again, and she never did.

Suggested reading: Minnie Buce Carrigan, *Captured by the Indians* (Privately published from a serial account in *The Buffalo Lake News* in January, 1903, no date).

Public Execution in Mankato

TRAVELING WEST

Eleven-year-old Martin Mahoney started west for California in 1859 with his older brothers, Thomas, fifteen, and Jerry, the oldest (we don't know his age). We don't know where they were from. Here is a letter Martin wrote to his sister, Mary, after he reached California.

"My Dear Sister Mary:

"I am afraid you will go nearly crazy when you read my letter. If Jerry has not written you before now, you will be surprised to hear that we are in California, and that poor Thomas is dead.

"We started in July with plenty of provisions and too yoke of oxen. We went along very well till we got within six or seven hundred miles of California, when the Indians attacked us. We found places where they had killed the emigrants. We had one passenger with us, too guns, and one revolver; so we ran all the lead we had into bullets and hung the guns up in the wagon so that we could get at them in a minit. It was about two o'clock in the afternoon; droave the cattel a little way; when a prairie chicken alited a little way from the wagon.

"Jerry took out one of the guns to shoot it and told Tom to drive the oxen. Tom and I drove the oxen, and Jerry and the passenger went on. Then, after a little, I left Tom and caught up with Jerry and the other man. Jerry stopped for Tom to come up; me and the man went on and sit down by a little stream.

"In a few minutes we heard some noise; then three shots (they all struck poor Tom, I suppose); then they gave the war hoop, and as many as twenty of the red skins came down upon us. The three that shot Tom was hid by the side of the road in the bushes.

"I thought Tom and Jerry were shot; so I told the other man that Tom and Jerry were dead, and that we had better try and escape if possible.

"I had no shoes on; having a sore foot, I thought I would not put them on. The man and me run down the road, but we was soon stopt by an Indian on a pony. We then turend the other way and run up the side of the mountain and hid behind some cedar trees, and stayed there until dark.

"The Indians hunted all over after us, and verry close to us, so close that we could here there tomyhawks jingle. At dark the man and me started on, I stubing my toes against sticks and stones. We traveld on all night; and the next morning, just as it was getting gray, we saw something in the shape of a man. It layed down in the grass. We went up to it, and it was Jerry. He thought we ware Indians.

"You can imagine how glad he was to see me. He thought we was all dead but him, and we thought him and Tom was dead. He had the gun that he took out of the wagon to shoot the prairie chicken; all he had was the load that was in it.

"We traveld on till about eight o'clock. We caught up with one wagon with too men in it. We had traveld with them before one day; we stopt and they drove on; we knew that they was ahead of us, unless they had been killed to. My feet was so sore when we caught up with them that I had to ride; I could not step.

"We traveld on for too days, when the men that owned the cattle said they could not drive them another inch. We unyoked the oxen; we had about seventy pounds of flour; we took it out and divided it into four packs.

"Each of the men took about 18 pounds apiece and a blanket. I carried a little bacon, dried meat, and little quilt; I had in all about twelve pounds. We had one pint of flour a day for our alloyance. Sometimes we made soup of it; sometimes we made pancakes; and sometimes mixed it up with cold water and eat it that way.

"We traveld twelve or fourteen days. The time came at last when we should have to reach someplace or starve. We saw fresh horse and cattle tracks. The morning came, we scraped all the flour out of the sack, mixed it up, and baked it into bread, and made some soup, and eat everything we had. We traveld on all day without anything to eat, and that evening we caught up with a sheep train of eight wagons. We traveld with them until we arrived at the settlements; and know I am safe in California, and got to good home, and going to school.

"Jerry is working. It is a good country. You can get from 50 to 60 and 75 dollars for cooking. Tell me all about the affairs in the States, and how all the folks get along."

The Mary who received the letter later moved to San Francisco. Robert Louis Stevenson, the Scottish writer, rented a room from her and she gave him the letter. We don't know what happened to Martin, but he must have died in his early twenties. He was long since dead in 1879, when his sister gave Stevenson the letter.

Suggested reading: Robert Louis Stevenson, *From Scotland to Silverado* (Cambridge: Harvard University Press, 1966).

FAMILY CIRCLE

E meline Trimble, 13-year-old daughter of Abagail Utter's first marriage,
remembered the sorrow of their 1860 parting from Wisconsin
neighbors to go to Oregon:

"Although tears were in our eyes at the thought of parting, still we
were hopeful, for we dearly loved each other, stepfather, stepbrothers and
sisters all being united and happy, and the thought that in that far land to
which we were to go, we would be so fortunate as to live an unbroken
family in nice homes, near father and mother, and if the Lord will it, with
not a face missing in our family circle, gave strength to pass through the
sorrowful parting."

It was a large family circle: Abagail's three, Elijah's six and their own
Susan who would be one on September 10.

They were joined by neighbors Joe and Mary Myers and their five
children.

Other wagons joined along the trail. When they reached the soda
springs in August where the California-bound wagons turned southwest,
eight wagons continued on to the abandoned trade post at Fort Hall. These
included, besides the Utter and Myers families, the Chase family from
Illinois (Daniel and Elizabeth and their three children), the Van Ornum
family from Wisconsin (Alexis and Abigail with their five children), and
some single men.

Elijah Utter was elected captain of the Oregon-bound train. A 22-
man army escort from the 2nd Dragoons traveled with the train for six days
from Fort Hall. Five recently-discharged soldiers going to Oregon also
joined the train. After the escort turned back, the emigrants discovered that
a young soldier had deserted. He was allowed to remain with the train.

On September 4, the train left the main Oregon Trail and continued
along the south bank of the Snake River. They reached Castle Creek on
Saturday, September 8. That night Indians stole two of the Van Ornum
oxen.

The next day the discharged soldiers rode ahead and saw a war party
of about one hundred Indians — Shoshones or Bannocks — most of them on
foot. Elijah Utter ordered the wagons corralled for defense. The Indians
charged, waving their blankets and shouting war-whoops. For the rest of her
life Emeline Trimble would flinch whenever she heard a shrill yell.

The emigrants had eighteen men and boys with weapons, five
women, and twenty-one children aged fourteen and younger.

After an hour's battle, the Indians threw down their weapons, made
the peace sign, and said they would go away if they were fed. A majority

of the men thought it prudent to buy the Indians' favor with food.

After the Indians were fed and the wagons were strung out along the trail, the Indians ambushed them. By the time Utter got the wagons corralled, three emigrant men had been killed. More and more Indians joined the attackers.

The day was very hot, and the emigrants had not filled their extra water kegs as they expected to be traveling close to the river that day. The plaintive cries of the little children made the fighting men realize that they had more to worry about than marksmanship. Some of the cows had milk and they gave it to the babies. Only the very young children were able to sleep that first night.

The fighting renewed at daybreak, little Susan Utter's first birthday. Another man was killed this day; Dan Chase and Elijah Utter were both wounded. None of the men had had anything to eat or drink after the second attack on Sunday. They had fought half of Sunday, all night, and all day Monday. The women and children loaded the guns and handed them to the men and older boys as they fought from shallow trenches they had dug. Listening to the pitiful cries of thirsty children, the men decided to make a run for it.

They would take one wagon for each family, leaving the other four, hoping the booty would satisfy the Indians. The three surviving ex-soldiers and the deserter volunteered to ride ahead as skirmishers.

It didn't work. The Indians attacked, paying no attention to the wagons left behind. The four soldiers spurred the horses they had been given and escaped, leaving the emigrants to their fate. They also carried away the extra rifles and revolvers which the emigrants had provided to them.

The emigrants killed about thirty Indians, ten of them by twelve-year-old Charles Utter, Emeline's step brother. Emeline, blind in one eye from an earlier injury, helped defend their wagon with an axe.

Then the Indians crowded in, jumped on the wagons, and began ripping their canvas covers to get inside. Joe Myers knew that his brother had been killed. He shouted at his wife, "Get out Mary, and we'll try to all die together."

As he helped Mary down, a bullet passed through Joe, striking Mary in the breast, and she fell dead. Joe did his best to gather their five children around him.

Elijah Utter was holding little Susan, the birthday baby. Emeline took the child so her stepfather could shoot better. Just then Mary Utter, Emeline's 23-year-old stepsister, was shot and killed. Elijah put down his rifle and tried to tell the Indians they could have everything if they would only let the survivors go.

As Abagail Utter bent over her dying stepdaughter, Elijah was shot. He fell dead beside his daughter Mary. By now Emeline was running with Susan in her arms and five-year-old Wesley Utter at her side. She called her mother to follow, but Abagail refused to leave her husband. Wesley and his two little sisters ran to Abagail. Then the thirteen-year-old girl, still holding baby Susan in her arms, persuaded her three stepbrothers and stepsister to try and escape with her.

The Indians, perhaps satisfied that they had killed enough adults, began looting the train, and Emeline got away with her little brood of four.

The twenty-seven still alive of the original forty-four decided to stay away from the trail and the river. They found a small stream, drank their fill, rested, and traveled until daylight. Once, when Indians passed near, Baby Susan began crying at the frightened faces around her. Emeline, with an aching heart, held her hand over the baby's mouth to stifle the cries.

After four nights, they began traveling by day and camping at night. Three nights later they killed and ate one of the two dogs that had followed them. They ate rosebuds, berries, and roots, and sometimes caught fish. After they had eaten the second dog, they ate a rattlesnake. They killed a cow which was apparently trying to return home from a train in front of them. They ate the tough, stringy flesh and even charred the bones in fire so they could be eaten. By mixing the cow's flesh with rosebuds, they made it last two weeks.

About the middle of September, ten-year-old Christopher Trimble and Goodsel Munson, an old man, were sent ahead to see if they could find help. Five days later they came upon the 18-year-old deserter, still mounted on one of the Van Ornum horses, and two other men who had escaped earlier. When the three men learned the people were starving, they killed and roasted the horse. Then they and the old man went on ahead, hoping to reach Fort Walla Walla and send back help.

Christopher trudged back nineteen miles, carrying all the horsemeat he could to the other emigrants. He found them stopped, unable to travel further. They were building brush shelters near the Owyhee River, a few miles from its intersection with the Snake. They thought they had traveled about ninety miles from where they were first attacked.

They had no blankets and little clothing. They ate lizards, frogs, snakes, and mussels from the Owyhee River, near which they had set up their camp.

About October first, after they had been in their camp about two weeks, the emigrants were discovered by Shoshone Indians. The Indians were drying salmon from the fall run in the Snake River. These Indians appeared peaceful. They traded fresh-caught salmon for clothing, until the emigrants were almost naked. The Indians liked Christopher Trimble and invited him to their camp for a few days. The fearless ten-year-old, rested from his long trip carrying horsemeat, said he would go. Emeline protested, but the boy said if they refused to let him come back he would just run away next summer when another emigrant train came through.

The Indians brought Christopher back in three days as they promised. In the meantime, Mr. Chase had died from overeating the fish traded from the Indians, and the Van Ornum family had moved on. They took Charles and Henry Utter with them, but refused to take Emeline, Baby Susan, or the younger Trimble children.

Christopher Trimble went back again with the Indians to their camp. He said they had treated him well, and had given him plenty to eat.

But the Indians became more insolent, robbed the remaining men of their guns, and made no more visits. Emeline worried about Christopher.

Soon the survivors, many nearly naked after trading clothing for food, were huddled over their fires, starving to death. They apparently made no attempt to fish in the nearby rivers. They ate moss, grass, and weeds, and any dead animals they could find.

The Myers family and Mrs. Chase argued about dividing food between parents and their children. Mrs. Chase thought the Myers were starving themselves too much to feed more to the children. She thought if the adults died first, the children would be left to the wolves. Joe and Mary Myers thought Mrs. Chase was selfish in how she divided with her children.

Nine-year-old Libby Trimble died while she and sister Emeline were gathering fuel. Within an eight-day period Baby Susan and the two young Chase children also starved to death.

After much discussion and some prayers, the survivors decided to eat the flesh from the four recently-starved children. A few days later Mr. Myers found where wolves had dragged something across the path between the shelters and the Shoshone camp on the Snake River. He followed, hoping to find the carcass of a deer. What he found were two locks of hair which Emeline recognized as Christopher's.

Myers did find the carcass of a horse, stripped to the bones by coyotes or wolves. They carried it into the camp and roasted the bones and skin.

They discovered that Mr. Chase's body had been dug up and stripped of clothing by the Indians. On October 24, the survivors cut the corpse into small pieces, roasted them, and were about to eat when they saw Emeline, who had been out looking for rosebuds, staggering toward them. She was pointing toward the west and trying to scream something.

What Emeline saw was an army rescue party, organized after one of the discharged soldiers had reached a camp in the Blue Mountains. The survivors tried to run to the soldiers, but they fell to the ground, weeping and trying to shout in their joy.

The soldiers, all weeping themselves, grabbed for their rations. The officer in charge shouted, "Stop, you'll kill them if they overeat."

The soldiers fed each adult and most of the children a few mouthfuls of food. Every two hours they gave them a little soup and coffee.

The Myers baby almost died, although she was only given a few drops of a weak gruel. The soldiers worked all night to keep her alive. Her five-year-old brother had no desire for food. His eyes were glazed over. The soldiers kept him warm, forcing gruel into his mouth from time to time. They thought none of the children would live more than three days.

The soldiers helped the women make skirts from army blankets, and they shared their coats — even their underclothing — with the survivors.

They started the return march on October 27 in a heavy sleet storm. Four children rode in hampers on pack mules. Two rode with their mothers on mule litters. None of the women were able to ride alone. One sat on a mule, with two soldiers walking alongside to keep her from falling off. The others rode on litters made from blankets, stretched between pairs of mules.

In early November the party met the ambulances that had been sent from Fort Walla Walla. Now the people had warm clothing and comfortable wagons to ride in.

The army found the Van Orman party, all killed by Indians.

Emeline went to live with her uncle in Oregon. All the other people in her family circle were now dead. She was a brave 13-year old girl. One-fourth of her genes came from grandfather Christopher Columbus Trimble, Indian-fighting hero of both the War of 1812 and the Blackhawk War. He would have been proud of Emeline and her brother, Christopher.

Suggested reading: Donald Shannon, *The Utter Disaster on the Oregon Trail* (Caldwell: Snake Country Pub. 1993).

TWICE ABANDONED

The small wagon train captained by Josiah Kelly had just crossed Horseshoe Creek near present Casper, Wyoming, when the Oglala Sioux attacked at dusk on July 12, 1864. The seven men, two women, and two children in the five-wagon train were outnumbered ten to one. After three men had been killed and two wounded, Josiah shouted for the others to run and hide in the sage brush.

"Our best chance is to get some army help, follow their trail, and get our women and children back," he told the others.

Left behind were Josiah's wife, Fanny, her niece Mary, and Sarah Larimer, and her son Frank. Both children were about seven years old.

The Indians loaded Fanny and Mary on one captured horse (it was Mr. Larimer's) and Sarah and Frank on another. They headed north.

After traveling a few miles, it was completely dark. Fanny spoke softly to Mary, saying, "When I find a good place, I'll help you slip down. You lie perfectly still until daylight. Then you follow our trail back to the emigrant trail and someone will come along and see you. I'll try to follow if I get a chance. Be sure you don't move, my little daring."

Mary nodded, her eyes wide with fear, and did as she was told.

When Fanny slipped down later, the Indians saw her riderless horse and soon found her. She persuaded them that Mary had fallen asleep and fallen off. She said she had tried to tell them and had finally got down to search for the girl.

The Indians apparently believed her, but were unable to find Mary.

The next day three or four soldiers were riding west when they saw Mary on a distant bluff. They had been chased by Indians the day before, and they feared the girl was a decoy, placed by the Indians to lead them into an ambush. When they saw Indians in the ravine separating them from Mary, they turned and fled to Deer Creek Station.

Another report says the soldiers heard the girl's plaintive cries for help, but did not see her. But, suspecting an ambush, they fled.

Josiah Kelly arrived at Deer Creek Station on foot after the fleeing soldiers rode in. He persuaded the station commander to send out a rescue party.

Little Mary, abandoned by her father and by the soldiers, was found dead. She lay face down, scalped, several arrows in her back, and her arms and hands stretched out as though imploring help from a protector.

Suggested reading: Fanny Kelly, *Narrative of My Captivity Among the Sioux Indians* (Hartford: Mutual Pub. Co., 1872).

38

JOURNEY TO ZION

Intense missionary work in northern Europe starting in the 1840s produced thousands of converts to the Mormon Church. The new Saints were encouraged to emigrate to the church's chosen homeland, Zion, in present Utah.

Religious zeal often proved stronger than family bonds. Sometimes one spouse converted and the other did not. More often, family poverty prevented all from going to Zion together, so families became separated and waited for reunion in Zion.

Brigham Roberts, five, and twelve-year-old Polly were left with their father in Lancashire, England, in 1862, when their mother and their older sister emigrated to Zion. The boy's first name suggests that his mother had waited at least five years for her journey to the chosen land.

Nine-year-old Brigham (usually called Harry) and Polly left Liverpool on the sailing vessel *John Bright*, on April 30, 1866. Harry does not mention his father; very likely the man did not convert.

The seven hundred Mormon passengers included many from Scotland and Wales. Harry remembered beautiful group singing with dancing and games on deck. The boys could even shoot marbles in calm weather. In fact, the only unpleasant memory he had of the voyage came from a marble game, when he refused to give back marbles he thought he had fairly won. "Blackeye," a sailor assigned to watch over the children, broke up a furious fist fight between Harry and John Gibbs, the boy who lost the marbles.

Harry did wonder why sixteen-year-old Polly cried so much upon leaving. For the boy it was a time of great joy, remembering how he had faithfully promised his mother to join her in Zion. He thought Polly was crying because she thought the ship would sink.

"Polly, this ship won't sink," he firmly assured her. She nodded tearfully.

While many Mormons wrote of near starvation with burials at sea for victims of disease, the *John Bright* apparently had a peaceful May crossing. It reached New York harbor on June 6.

Harry and his sister traveled by river boat, train, and covered wagon, arriving in the Salt Lake Valley on September 14. As they emerged from Emigration Canyon and traveled west on present Broadway to turn north toward Temple Square, Harry was proud to be in the lead.

Harry had no illusions about his appearance after the long trip from England. The trousers and jacket he had been wearing for five months had been made from the cast-off trousers of an English policeman. His freckled face had an upturned — almost misshapen — nose. Wide gaps in his ugly teeth allowed him to indulge in shrill whistles that were impossible for other boys. Harry was chunky of build, and his mouse-colored hair unkempt and unmanageable. His feet were cracked and blackened, although now covered with shoes that he had taken from a dead man back along the trail at a station that had been burned out by Indians.

People had turned out to welcome the new Saints, and Harry swaggered in the lead because he was tending the lead yoke of oxen on the captain's team. A brightly-dressed, dainty little girl stepped timidly into the street, a basket of fruit on her arm.

"Would you like some peaches?" she asked, unsure how close she should approach this strange-looking human.

Harry smiled and nodded. Without saying anything, he stacked as many peaches as he could along the crook of his arm. Polly, ashamed of her appearance, was hiding in a wagon behind. Harry hurried back, gave her the fruit, and then returned to his place at the head of the caravan.

When they reached Temple Square, Harry could see the foundations of the planned Temple, barely protruding above ground.

Large numbers of people had come to greet parents and children, spouses and sweethearts. But no one was there for Harry and Polly, still hiding in the wagon. Lonesome and heartsick, Harry sat on the tongue of the captain's wagon and thought that Zion was not so much after all, if that was all of it.

But soon, approaching from the west gate, he saw a woman in a red and white shawl, moving slowly between piles of manure that had been raked from the sheds and yard. As she daintily picked her way, searching to the right and left, there was something about her that seemed familiar to Harry. Finally he recognized her and jumped up, shouting, "Hey, Mother!"

She stopped, looked at him a long time without moving, and then asked, "Is that you, Harry? Where is Polly?"

He led his mother to the wagon where Polly hid, and tears flooded on both sides as they embraced each other. Once in a while, a smile would break through the tears momentarily as Ann Roberts realized that finally she had her children all together.

Ann's neighbor, Brother John Crosby of New England, had driven her in from Bountiful to meet the wagon train. Wonderful thoughts that he had finally arrived and belonged to somebody who had an interest in him filled Harry's heart and mind as the wagon moved north toward his new home.

Bountiful had a New England style meeting house with a large tower looming over the homes around it. Harry hoped that the tall building was his mother's new home. But when the wagon turned east and continued, he said nothing. Disappointment became humiliation when the wagon stopped two blocks past the meeting house. They had reached a small, unchinked log cabin with a dirt roof over one part and only the sky over the rest.

"Come with me, son," Ann said. "I haven't washed you for over four years."

She set up a wash tub and cloths in the unroofed part of the house. She stripped off the shirt Harry had been wearing since he left England and gave him a scrubbing that led Harry to wonder if she thought he had not once washed himself during the four years they had been apart.

Harry remembered the wonderful meal prepared by older sister, Annie. His desperately-poor mother could not afford much variety, but the preparation was fit for princes. They had light, buttermilk biscuits with butter, clear water from the creek, and a sweet, sticky something called "molasses."

They talked reunion far into the night. The next day, Harry's life in his new home began.

At age thirty-one, Harry became President of the First Council of the Seventy. A prolific writer of history and theology, he was elected to the United States Congress. He married three women and fathered fifteen children.

In the early 1880s, Harry was presiding over a mission in Tennessee. John Gibbs, the boy he had fought twenty years earlier over the marbles on the ship, and, at one time a member of the Tennessee mission, had been martyred to the faith of the Latter Day Saints. At some risk to himself, Harry brought John's body from Tennessee back to his hometown in Utah for burial.

Suggested reading: Susan A. Madsen and Fred E. Woods, *I Sailed to Zion* (Salt Lake City: Desert Book Co., 2000.)

BRIGHAM (HARRY) ROBERTS

Utah State Historical Society

KIOWA CAPTIVE

Aperian Crow of the Kiowa tribe had practically everything a person could want. A noted war chief, he was a member of the Koitsenko society, elected by the tribe as its ten bravest. A superb hunter with high status and great wealth in horses, he could give his wife, Medicine Hunt Girl, the finest clothing, the finest tipi. They had everything but what they wanted most of all. They had no children!

On October 13, 1864, seven hundred Comanche and Kiowa warriors raided into Texas in the largest Indian raid of the Civil War. Little Buffalo of the Comanches and Aperian Crow led the raid. Little Buffalo lost his life. Aperian Crow found his chid.

She was Millie Durgan, eighteen months old. Aperian Crow found her hiding under the bed at her grandmother's ranch after the warriors killed her mother and a twelve-year-old boy. They captured Millie, her sister, her grandmother, and four others and rode back north, leaving eleven dead settlers behind.

The delighted chief presented Millie to his wife, who shared his joy at their great blessing. The lovely white-skinned girl would be raised, not as a slave, but as their own foster daughter!

The next month the Kiowas attacked a large force of soldiers under Kit Carson in the first Battle of Adobe Walls. Families went along on this raid, and Medicine Hunt Girl hid their new daughter in the grass during the battle.

The foster parents cherished their daughter. They kept her face painted dark and insisted that the tribe conceal her presence from whites. Within a year all the captives taken in the Texas raid, except one boy — killed because he couldn't keep up with the returning raiders — had been sold back to the whites. But the tribe never revealed that they had the little girl.

In later years Millie's grandmother searched for her, but the Kiowas kept the secret. Millie's new parents told her early that she was white and adopted. But always being hidden when whites came around, made her grow up fearful of her own race.

Millie and her new mother had the best of everything. Millie wore the finest clothing and rode the best horses. She learned all the domestic duties expected of an Indian woman. She cooked meat just as her parents liked it, and she could tan hides well. She was particularly good at handling livestock. Once some men and boys chased a frightened deer into the camp. It was lashing out with sharp front feet when Millie dived in, grabbed its legs, and threw it to the ground. She claimed a hind quarter as the first person to touch the animal.

When Aperian Crow was deathly ill, Millie sought help from a medicine woman. The chief recovered after the medicine woman's incantations. A grateful Millie gave the medicine woman a fine colt which Aperian Crow had given to Millie. The colt later became a famous race horse.

Medicine Hunt Girl guarded her daughter carefully. Millie was not allowed to go to sun dance festivals with young men, one of the few times that Kiowa girls could date. "She is not like the rest of you," her mother told the boys.

Millie married Goombie a fine young man from an honored family. He served as a government scout. They had nine children. When Goombie died, Millie married his cousin, honoring the Kiowa custom of a widow marrying a kinsman so she could care for his children, as well as her own.

Millie grew up in the Indian faith. She believed in the Grandmother Gods and the sacred Taime. Not until all her children had become Christian did Millie agree to even consider the new faith.

At her children's urging, Millie also agreed to learn what she could of her blood relatives. She was sixty-nine before she found out who she was. But she always considered herself an Indian, lucky to have been raised by such devoted foster parents.

Millie lived a full and happy life. She died at the home of a daughter. She was buried in the reservation cemetery at Rainy Mountain, Oklahoma. Those attending the funeral included relatives, both red and white, army officers, and pioneers who remembered the raid where she had been captured seventy-two years before.

Suggested reading: Mildred P. Mayhall *Indian Wars of Texas* (Waco: Texian Press, 1965).

LAURA

Laura was born on a cold February day in 1867 in a log cabin overlooking the Mississippi River, near Pepin, Wisconsin. Her parents worked hard in the woods, Pa hunting, fishing, and clearing trees for farmland, Ma gardening, making clothing, and putting up food for winter.

Ma liked to stay settled in places with schools and churches, but Pa was restless, always wanting to move west to better land. They both wanted the best for their daughters, Mary and Laura.

Laura didn't remember their first move; she was not yet two. Pa and Ma's brother Henry, who had married Pa's sister, each bought eighty acres of Missouri prairie land. They loaded their families into covered wagons and headed south.

For some reason, both families moved again the next year. Uncle Henry returned to the big woods in Wisconsin. But Pa and Ma went further southwest. They crossed the Verdigris River in southeastern Kansas, and passed through a settlement of log and sod shacks which called itself Independence. Ma saw this sign in front of a cabin: "Bred and Pize for Saile Huar." But Pa wanted to go out on the open prairie, away from too much settlement. So they traveled thirteen miles further, stopping near Walnut Creek in present Montgomery County.

Pa built a small log cabin, dug a well, and started breaking sod. Little sister Carrie was born there in 1870.

Laura and Mary enjoyed playing in the creek bottoms, watching hawks overhead — sometimes soaring high, sometimes diving low for a furry meal — following deer tracks, and watching for snakes. In late summer and fall they would lie in their beds and listen to the mournful songs of cowboys trailing Texas cattle to the railroad.

But the prairie had its own hardships. Ma and Pa got malaria from mosquitos. Pa had innocently built their cabin on land belonging to the Osage Indians, who resented the invading settlers. There were also wolves in winter and prairie fires in summer.

When Gust Gustafson, the buyer of their Wisconsin property, wrote that he wanted to give it back and head west himself, Pa and Ma loaded their growing family into the wagon and returned to the Wisconsin woods.

They were glad to be back with relatives, and Laura loved the cozy winter nights with a glowing fire and Pa playing his beautiful, honey-brown violin. The music he coaxed from the instrument filled the small rooms, etching itself in Laura's memory.

Ma had insisted that the girls not speak at the table unless spoken to and to always remember their manners. She also wanted them to attend school whenever possible. Back in Wisconsin, Mary got to go to school, and Laura felt lonely with only baby Carrie at home. But once Laura was invited to visit school for a whole day! It was particularly exiting to hear Mary speak the piece before the whole room that she had memorized at home. Laura remembered the long hours Mary had struggled to commit it to memory. That fall Laura was four, and she started to school.

Ma, who had been a teacher, often read aloud in her soft, low voice, and Laura listened carefully. How she wanted to tell fascinating stories like Ma read on those long winter evenings!

When Laura was almost seven, Pa was ready to move again. The Big Woods was filling up with settlers and game was getting scarce. Another brother, Peter, had also married another of Ma's sisters. Pa and Peter wanted to go west where they did not have to dig out stumps to make farmland. Again the covered wagons were loaded and goodbyes said.

Peter's family stopped on Minnesota's Zumbro River, but Pa kept going west to Plum Creek near Walnut Station at the edge of the Minnesota prairies. Laura remembered the rabbits, the meadowlarks, and the prairie chickens, and how whole villages of gophers darted about, flicking their tails in the sunshine.

This time they lived in a dugout, excavated into a creek bank. The roof of the dugout was made from willow branches, hay, and sod. Laura enjoyed standing on it and imagining it was part of the grassy prairie, stretching away to the horizon. Ma soon had the dugout clean and homey with smooth, whitewashed dirt walls. Laura loved to swim in Plum Creek and pick juicy wild plums along its banks.

Pa worked for neighbor Eleck Nelson until he had enough money to buy a cow. Laura enjoyed visiting with Alena Nelson, and her mother, Anna, who taught her how to milk. When Pa brought the new cow home, Laura surprised her family with her new, practical skill.

Laura and Mary were enrolled in school in Walnut Station, and Ma and Pa helped establish the Congregational Church there. Pa became a trustee in the church. The Pastor was a Vermonter who had graduated from Dartmouth and a seminary in Maine. He came west at the service of the American Home Missionary Society.

The next spring, Pa built a house of lumber on the banks of the creek, and they moved out of the dark dugout which often dripped mud from the roof long after the rains stopped. Sometimes even snakes and lizards dropped in uninvited.

But in summer 1875 a terrible cloud of grasshoppers came down from the Minnesota sky and destroyed Pa's beautiful wheat crop. Leaving his stripped fields behind, he walked east following the railroad tracks to find harvest work for others who had escaped the infestation. In October they moved into town as Ma was expecting again, and Pa wanted to be closer to help if it was needed. Baby Freddie arrived in November.

Pa planted wheat again in 1876, but the grasshoppers hatched out as the new wheat came up from the rich soil, and they knew there would not be a harvest that year, either. By now Laura was nine, a spirited, independent, intelligent girl who, like Pa, felt the enticing call of the West.

Pa, Ma, and the four children loaded back into the covered wagon and returned to the Mississippi River to stay with Uncle Peter in Wabasha County. There, at nine months of age, Freddie died suddenly. Laura remembered that awful day, Sunday, August 27, when he "straightened out his little body and was dead." Never again would Laura be able to hold her sweet, tiny brother in her arms. Devastated, the family mourned together and moved on to Iowa to run a hotel. Baby Grace was born there in 1877.

The family didn't like hotel work, so they loaded the wagon back up and returned to Walnut Station. Laura was now eleven.

Then older sister Mary became gravely ill in winter 1879. Her high fever brought delirium. She recovered slowly but lost her eyesight. Pa asked Laura to describe things for Mary so she wouldn't feel left out.

Laura remembered how Mary had ridden the covered wagon, her sunbonnet neatly tied under her chin, her blue eyes darting back and forth as she watched the wild, unspoiled grasslands. Now Mary depended on Laura to describe what she could no longer see.

Laura thought those descriptions were the beginning of her interest in writing. She had always wanted to tell stories like Ma, but now she wanted to tell them so well the hearer or reader could see as though actually present.

Then Pa moved further west into Dakota Territory, where he worked first at railroad building and then filed a homestead claim in Spring 1880. He promised Ma it would be their last move.

Laura loved the challenge of homesteading, particularly building their tarpaper claim shack and the haying. She also helped Ma in the garden, looked after the younger girls, and patiently described the beauty of the prairie to Mary.

In 1882 Laura, now fifteen, began teaching in a one-room school. Sixteen was the minimum age for teachers, but the School Board conveniently forgot to ask Laura about that detail.

Soon Almanzo, a local homesteader, who had grown up on a farm in New York, came courting. They married in 1885 when Laura was eighteen, and moved to their own homestead claim, a few miles away.

As the years went on, Laura and Almanzo had two children, one dying in infancy. Their house burned to the ground and they moved to Florida and back again, finally settling in the Missouri Ozarks. Almanzo became partially paralyzed after he had diphtheria. Their daughter Rose, named for the wild roses that brightened the prairies in spring, became a noted author. Laura, too, began writing.

As she sat at the beautiful writing desk Almanzo had made, she remembered how Pa had sat so tall on the wagon seat, whistling cheerily as he urged the horses forward. She remembered Ma sitting beside Pa and holding baby Carrie or baby Freddie or baby Grace. Always they headed west where the prairie was new and free and clean, and lay waiting for hard-working settlers to make new homes there.

Her first book was published when Laura was sixty-five. Several more followed. They told about living in a covered wagon on the move. They vividly brought to light Mary's blindness, Pa's singing violin, Ma's story telling, and Alanzo's patient, hard work.

Little House on the Prairie and the others are crowded with warm love, deep faith, inner courage, and the patient strength that carried Laura Ingalls Wilder and her family through sickness, death, fire, storms, and grasshoppers, leaving the family stronger after each encounter. Laura lived the experiences, and she described them so readers almost lived them, too. Her nine "Little House" books have become priceless chronicles of pioneer life.

Suggested reading: Donald Zochert, *Laura, the Life of Laura Ingalls Wilder* (New York: Avon Books, 1976).

QUICK DEATH IN SAN QUENTIN

Harvey Mitchell, a Pomo Indian, left home to work for a white family in Cloverdale, California, when he was very small. Some years later — in summer 1871 — Harvey, barely thirteen, moved to the Charles Brown home. There he heard brothers Lodi and Johnny Brown talk about their robberies of stagecoaches. Harvey decided that he could get ahead faster in crime than in hard work for white families.

On the following Christmas night Harvey crept into the bushes a mile south of Geyserville, waiting for the stage to Healdsburg. In his hands he clutched a redwood picket that he had whittled down to resemble a rifle. Doc Curtis was driving the stage that night.

Curtis liked to brag about what he would do if robbers tried to hold him up. "If them knights of the road try to hang me up," he often said, "they'll never get another chance, you bet."

Curtis slowed to go around a downed tree and the thirteen-year-old Indian boy stepped out with his crude rifle. "Throw down the box," he ordered. Curtis wasted no time doing just that.

When Curtis reached Healdsburg he told how he had stared into the twin barrels of a shotgun for some time before he handed down the box.

Harvey dragged the box into the brush and opened it with a dull axe. Unfortunately for his new career, it was empty.

Within days Harvey was arrested. After a one-day trial in early January, he was found guilty and sentenced to a year in San Quentin. At that time the prison had one of the worst reputations in United States prisons, particularly for sexual abuse. Admitting Harvey — at thirteen, its youngest inmate ever — was throwing a lamb to the wolves.

When Harvey was released in November, he continued in his new career of crime. He returned to San Quentin on a one-year burglary sentence when he was eighteen.

Five days after his next prison release, Harvey was again arrested for burglary. Back in San Quentin for the third time, the Indian boy — just five days past his twentieth birthday — died. No cause of death was given. Perhaps it was despair.

Suggested reading: Mark Dugan, *The Making of Legends* (Athens: Swallow Press, 1997).

MONT HAWTHORNE'S PLEDGE

I was eleven when I took the pledge," recalled Mont Hawthorne as he talked to his niece. "Pa and I was about to leave with two wagons for the Black Hills from our homestead on the Middle Loup River in Nebraska. It was early spring in seventy-seven. Mama took me aside and told me some things that I had suspicioned about. One of them was that Pa did too much drinking from time to time. In fact, he wasn't home yet, and we was leaving in a big wagon train the very next morning.

"'Looks like you're near a man, and not even twelve yet,' Mama said. 'Reckon you know there's good women and some's not so good.' I didn't let on, but I knew what she was getting at.

"Mama was a practical nurse, you know. She helped women have their babies."

"I know, Uncle Mont." The niece smiled at another story coming.

"'A boy been around cows as much as you should know about blood lines,' Mama said. 'If bulls are let run wild, you won't have a good calf in the pasture.'

"I knew Mama had nursed women who'd worked at the only business they knowed because they needed her when the babies came. She seen how hard it was when they didn't have a man standing by — and generally not even knowing who the father was. She knew I was dead set on seeing the world and she didn't quarrel with that; she just didn't want me leaving no unpaid debts along the trail. She said it wasn't as easy to start a fire and then try to put it out as it was to shut the damper before the fire got out of the stove. 'Some day you'll meet someone,' she said, 'and that's when you'll be wanting a clean mind in a clean body. You'll never make that girl happy if you let strong drink get the upper hand and come between you.'

"Then she told me about the Apostle Paul and what he thought about the place of women. She'd looked into it and she thought the laws of Nebraska were even harder on women than the teachings of Paul.

"Well, anyway, I always remembered what Mama said and I never broke the pledge I took that night. I took some teasing about it, but I never broke it."

Suggested reading: Martha F. McKeown, *Them Was The Days* (Lincoln: University of Nebraska Press, 1961).

STORIES TO TELL AT SCHOOL

Ten-year-old Walt Coburn idolized older half-brother Wallace. Wallace was a real cowboy on their father's Circle C Ranch in the Little Belt Mountains of Montana.

Young Walt carried Bull Durham in his shirt pocket, proudly rolling his own smokes. The Climax chewing tobacco in his hip pocket usually made him sick, but Wallace never laughed. Walt knew he could cuss and recite bawdy verses from The Old Chisholm Trail as much as he liked when Wallace was around as his audience. And he had learned many verses from Texas cowhands coming to Montana.

In late August in the late 1890s, Walt had looked forward to riding in the fall roundup before taking the train to Great Falls for another year of elementary school. The roundup was postponed, but Wallace saved the day when he invited his disappointed little brother to help trail home some cattle from a ranch on the Missouri River which their father had just bought. It would take two weeks.

They pulled out before sunup, leading two packhorses behind their mounts. They reached Tex Alford's log cabin saloon as darkness was falling. A half-breed hay crew, putting up hay on the Coburn ranch, was also there. They lined up at the bar, and Tex gave Walt and two young boys in the hay crew a quart of beer each.

"Now remember, Walt," Wallace cautioned, "that's all you get. When you down that one, you go on the Injun list — no more beer for you."

Walt and the half-breed boys enjoyed drinking up. After their meal they sat around the bonfire and listened to Wallace tell of his days in the Montana vigilantes. He told of hanging five rustlers at once, and chills shivered down Walt's young spine.

The weather had turned cold by the time they reached the cattle. They started the herd before daybreak, and Walt, riding back with the drags, wondered if the sun would ever come out. His threadbare overalls and thin summer shirt were little protection against the biting wind. By noon a cold drizzle had turned to snow. How Walt wished he had brought a warm jacket!

The trail crew consisted of Walt, Wallace, and four men from the ranch their father had bought. All the men had longjohns, sheepskin coats and slickers. That first afternoon trailing the cattle, Walt and his brother rode over to the cabin of a Circle C wolfer, which was vacant with this sign on the door:

THE LAST CAMP ROBBIN SON OF A BITCH WHO STOLE MY GRUB DIED OF STRICKNINE POISON

Wallace pushed the cabin door open and entered carefully, probing ahead with a broom. Walt waited expectantly, and walked in after he heard the loud noise of the jagged steel jaws of the heavy wolf trap snapping shut.

They got a warm fire going which brought out a strong stench from coyote and wolf pelts hanging on all four walls. Then Wallace collected a flannel shirt, long wool socks, a heavy wool undershirt, and a pair of matching drawers from the six feet six wolfer's inside clothes line. Using a heavy shears, a harness needle, and coarse black thread, he made a suit of underwear for Walt, who weighed all of seventy-five pounds if he had his pockets full of rocks. Walt was now warm at last, but he had to take short steps when he walked.

Wallace left a ten dollar bill and a note for the wolfer about the supplies he had used.

Walt rode into the home ranch on Sunday, and he knew he'd have to catch the morning stage to Malta and the night train to Great Falls to reach school in time.

Ranch cook Al Taylor agreed to give Walt a haircut provided he had a bath first. When Al cut the boy out of his makeshift underwear, he said, "Lord a mercy, what ails you kid? You're done broke out all over. You must be comin' down with measles!"

"I been scratchin' myself for days," Walt said. Must be that undershirt Wallace sewed me up in so tight."

Al examined the undershirt. "You're lousy as a pet coon." He dropped the garment in the iron barrel used to burn trash.

Al gave the boy a hard scrubbing with kerosene water and yellow lye soap.

The next morning Walt boarded the stage, wearing a short hair cut and still smelling of kerosene with a heavy overlay of bay rum from the bunk house. But Walt had some good stories to tell the town kids at Whittier Grammar School in Great Falls.

Suggested reading: Walt Coburn, "A Lousy Ending to a Top-Notch Trail Drive," in *True West (February, 1970).*

HOMESTEAD MEMORIES

T oo many persons think sod shanties were like slum shacks in modern cities," said retired University of Colorado professor William J. Hazard. "Not so. I have fond memories of the shanty we moved to in 1879 in Polk County, northwestern Minnesota.

"Father lost his business in Fond du Lac, Wisconsin, in the 1879 depression. He and a cousin, Ambrose (Amby) Blatchley, went west and filed on adjoining quarter sections. They built a sixteen by sixteen foot shanty across the boundary between the claims so that living there would satisfy the residence requirement for each claim.

"Father traded work with neighbors for the use of a yoke of oxen and a breaking plow. He and Amby built a lumber shack with battens over the cracks and enclosed it with sod walls and a sod roof. Then they built a small barn with sod walls and a roof of straw laid over poles and held down with more poles and rocks.

"They finished in late fall, and father returned to Wisconsin to start a new job writing county histories to earn money over the winter. Mother, my older sister Vessie who was thirteen, and I went to the new home by train. The last part of the journey was on an 'accomodation train,' a freight with a passenger car or two added.

"I can still remember the immense flatness of the new land. Covered with snow, it looked like a giant, white pancake. A few coulees where melted snow collected every spring provided overnight rest to northbound ducks. Another Wisconsin family had homesteaded three miles west. I can remember standing outside, looking west and realizing that if my eyesight were only keener, I could see every rabbit, fox, skunk, and weasel between our place and theirs.

"Father and Amby had papered the walls to keep down the dust. They used the *Crookston Chronicle* and the *Polk County Journal.* I could already read, of course, but many children in those frontier shanties got their first practice in that art by reading the walls of their homes. We studied many ads for James Means' $2.50 shoes, Castoria, and Lydia Pinkham's Compound.

"The two beds and bureaus for Vessie and me took up the whole south wall. Mother stretched a curtain between so we each had a private room. We slept under heavy, warm buffalo robes.

"Our cellar was a hole under the house reached by a trap door in the middle of the floor. It had been dug with terraced steps running around the square, so it was all shelf space. We stored the canned fruit, vegetables and honey we had brought from Fond du Lac.

"The cookstove kept our house warm. We burned tamarack poles hauled from several miles east, along the Pembina Trail. We ate twice a day, breakfast about nine or ten, and dinner about four or five.

"We all had work to do. Amby sawed wood and shoveled snow and took care of our cow and chickens. Mother cooked, washed, sewed and mended, and cared for us. Once she nursed me through a long siege of something. She had a lot of home remedies — boneset, tansy, saffron, and enderblow tea. She had little bottles with belladonna, nux, and pulsatilla, along with powdered rhubarb — a remedy for every ailment, I suppose.

"Vessie helped with the dishes and learned to sew. My job was to keep the wood box full and dig out hard blocks of snow for the wash boiler on the stove.   We both studied the few school books we had brought along.

"After dinner we amused ourselves playing euchre, old maid, and casino, as well as checkers and dominoes. We mixed in letter writing and singing songs to Amby's vigorous banjo accompaniment. Of course we played outside on warm days, building snow caves and following animal tracks.

"On one of those perfectly still mornings that first winter Mother reported that the thermometer had broken. She said the mercury had all leaked out. Amby found that the stem was only graduated to forty below. The mercury had merely taken refuge down in the bulb.

"I remember how happy we all were when spring came. Amby had been crippled in a boyhood accident with an axe, but he was active with his crutch. He danced a jig when we saw the icicles forming along the eaves as the snow started melting on the roof. Warm weather was on its way, and we looked forward to a new, exciting life on our homestead!"

Suggested reading: Forest Crossen, *Western Yesterdays* (Boulder: Boulder Publishing, Inc., 1967).

SAVED BY AN OLD INDIAN WOMAN

The last Indian raid in the Frio Canyon, north of Uvalde, Texas, happened on April 19, 1881. A group of Lipan Apaches ransacked the cabin of John McLaurin, who had settled on the West Fork of the Frio River, about eight miles north of present Leakey, Texas. McLaurin had left home that morning to go to Rio Frio, then known as "The Ditch," for supplies. Left at home were McLaurin's wife, Kate, age thirty-four, Allen Lease, a fifteen-year-old boy who worked for the family, and three small McLaurin children — Maud, five, Alonzo, three, and baby Frank. The oldest daughter, eight-year-old Mary, was boarding with a family in the settlements so she could attend school.

In mid afternoon Kate McLaurin, Allen Lease, Maud, and Alonzo had been setting out plants in the garden when Kate sat down on a blanket to nurse the baby. Just then she heard noises in the cabin, and, thinking the yard gate had been left open and the hogs were inside, she asked Allen to chase them out.

Allen ran up to the door and saw Indians raiding the cabin. He ran back down the hill toward Kate, and the Indians shot him in the back of the head, killing him instantly.

Kate jumped up, and the Indians shot her through the hips. She fell, but staggered back to her feet, shouting to Maud and Alonzo to run. Clutching the baby to her, Kate ran for the wooden fence at the edge of the clearing, trying to reach the river bottom. By the time she got over the fence, Kate had been shot four more times — in the left breast, in the right arm, and twice in the right leg.

Little Maud ran to the cabin to get a pillow for her mother, who lay bleeding from five wounds. She said one of the Indians grunted as he looked at her, but did not interfere, so the girl grabbed a pillow and ran back to her mother. Maud said several Indian men were stealing property from the cabin.

Maud made her mother as comfortable as she could, and Kate took Maud's bonnet, tore it into strips, and tried to bind her wounds.

Then Kate told Maud to run to the nearest cabin for help. On her way, Maud found a neighbor fishing in the river.

"Ma said to come," the little girl shouted as she gasped for breath. "The Indians shot her!"

The neighbor, a Mr. Fisher, ran home to get his gun and then to other neighbors for more help. They were surprised at the attack, as Indians had not raided there for several years.

Late in life, John McLaurin, wrote about "The Last Raid of Indeons," to his granddaughter, Margaret McLaurin Henderson. He said he saw the neighbors spreading the alarm as he came galloping down the trail. He may have had a hunch that something was wrong as he wrote, "I were riding fast as my mind carried me home."

McLaurin found his wife near sundown. She seemed to be asleep with Baby Frank lying close to her bloody breast. "I asked her if she wanted water," McLaurin wrote. "She said, 'yes.' I gave her water from my hat. After drinking, she only lived a short while."

About twenty men, including McLaurin's brother, followed the Indians' trail. All turned back except five who followed the trail west to the Nueces River. One of them rode on ahead to Fort Clark (present Brackettville) where he asked for help from Lieutenant John L. Bullis and his Seminole scouts.

The trail crossed the Rio Grande near present Del Rio. Bullis and his scouts followed it for five days into Mexico. One of their guides was an Indian woman who had been captured by a cowboy several years before. When she realized that she was following her own people, she tried unsuccessfully to throw the scouts off.

Bullis' army detail found the Lipans in the Santa Rosa mountains. They killed five men and one woman, and captured another old woman after wounding her child.

McLaurin's cabin had been stripped bare. The soldiers recovered some of the bedding and other household goods from the Lipans. John wrote: "They even taken grub from the house, as part of it was picked up by Henry Wall near home."

The old Indian woman, captured by Bullis, said the warriors would have killed the McLaurin children had it not been for her. She said she had been traveling regularly with this band of Indians. For about twenty years they had been making monthly raids into Texas to steal horses. They usually drove the horses north to Indian Territory for trade.

The four McLaurin children were all alive in 1929, when the account of the raid was written up by students in Leakey High School. Maud lived in San Antonio, the other children in Bell County, Texas. The students' spelling was a lot better than John McLaurin's, but the facts got changed a little in the re-telling.

Suggested reading: *Wagons, Ho! A History of Real County, Texas* (Curtis Media, Inc. 1995).

ANGIE CAHOON MEETS THE FAMILY MENFOLK

Angie Cahoon was born to Frances Evelyn Cahoon in Carthage, Dakota Territory, on August 2, 1888. The first child of Frances and her husband, George, Angie arrived in late afternoon after a long day of relatively easy labor. Several months before, Frances had asked George what he would like for his thirtieth birthday, which fell on August third.

"A kid," George answered.

Frances may have been thinking of that conversation when she mentioned, a few months before her confinement, that many important things had happened in the family on a Thursday.

"By Godfrey," George said, "that child'll be born on a Thursday, see if it ain't." He was right.

"Well, Mr. Cahoon, are you satisfied?" the doctor asked after Angie was born.

"Godfrey, yes!" George replied, "but I wish it had been a boy."

George had also hoped for a larger child. The baby weighed between six and seven pounds, but her father always said it was seven.

But George was soon almost worshiping the baby. When he came in from work, he would kiss Frances and go immediately to Angie, looking at her in a "perfect ecstacy of pride and delight." He would cover her with kisses and then laugh when Angie squinted up her face to get away from his rough beard. He washed out her first diapers.

George taught the baby to go to sleep in her own bed. The woman who was helping Frances had been rocking Angie to sleep, and George thought she should learn to go to sleep without being rocked. He would kneel in uncomfortable positions by her bed for two hours at a time — holding her little hands and laying his forehead against her rebellious head, in order to keep her quiet until fatigue brought sleep without the rocking.

George thought that children's bad habits should be subdued. It seemed to Frances that no man had ever been so patient with a child, yet so absolutely firm. He would spank the baby when she cried from temper and continue the spanking until It was evident that she was crying from the punishment and had forgotten the temper. Then the devoted father would soothe her by patting her and talking to her until she fell asleep.

George fell ill in November and died on Christmas day, before Angie's five-month birthday.

Frances' father came from New York to take his daughter and granddaughter to his family home. He hired a sleigh to transport Frances, her little sister who had been living with her, the baby, and their possessions to the train. Frances carried the baby outside and tried to hand her to Grandpa so she could climb into the sleigh. Grandpa shook his head and stepped back saying, "I don't know anything about babies." Later Frances wondered if she'd still be standing there had the driver not taken the baby so she could get in the sleigh.

Grandpa expected the baby to howl continually, and he preferred that the train passengers not know that he belonged to the family. He stayed in the smoking car at first. But as the journey progressed, he began spending more time with the rest of the family. Soon he worried that Angie wasn't getting enough to eat. Then he joyfully trotted back and forth to the stove, carrying the water needed for her diet of hot water, crackers, and sugar.

Toward the last of the journey, Grandpa wanted the other passengers to know that Angie was his grandchild. He took great pains to point out her good points to all who might be interested.

At first Angie was afraid of Frances' brother Ed. Ed had a loud voice, and when he spoke, the baby would cower against her mother or grandmother as though she had been struck. But Uncle Ed was very good to Angie. He held her as much as he could and enjoyed trotting with her in his arms. Soon Angie was warmly attached to her uncle.

Reading between the lines, it is apparent that Frances' parents were quite well to do. Angie soon became the center of every event in that home.

Frances' journal of the baby ended on Angie's first birthday. They had sat for a photograph but it had not been printed, as they could not find a ring for Angie of the correct size. But all was not a loss. "While we waited for the train to come home, Grandma went out and bought Angie a scrap book for pieces of her dresses. So she did have one present on her birthday."

Of course Angie, herself, had become a welcome present in that New York home.

Suggested reading: Elizabeth Hampsten, *Settlers' Children* (Norman: University of Oklahoma Press, 1991).

KIDNAPED ORPHANS

Father Constant Mandin, 25-year-old French priest, learned about the social division in the Clifton-Morenci community of Territorial Arizona soon after his arrival in February, 1904. The Sacred Heart Parish church was in Clifton, the oldest mining camp in the territory. Its forty-five hundred residents lived in narrow valleys, walled in by rocks and bluffs rising fifteen hundred feet higher. Their rough-built adobe homes and *jacalitos* (little shacks) on stilts were connected by dusty, manure-spotted streets except in times of flood. Morenci, five miles west and fifteen hundred feet higher, was similar except it was a company town, owned by Phelps Dodge. Store buildings were framed in wood, sometimes with stone veneers. Some of the larger homes of the Anglos were built of stone. But no one had running water, sewage disposal, or escape from the choking fumes at the copper smelter between the towns.

The majority of both towns were Mexican, but the Anglos had the best jobs, the best homes, the best opportunities, and got the best wages. The elementary schools had just begun to take in Mexican children, but most were taught at home. Most of Mandin's parishioners were Mexican. The Anglos had a small protestant church, not well attended.

A few months after his arrival in the new parish, Mandin got a letter from the New York Foundling Hospital about placing orphan children in Catholic homes in the West. He knew nothing about the hospital, the Sisters of Charity, or their work in placing orphans for adoption. But he recognized an opportunity to impress his bishop and to provide Catholic homes for orphans. Also, since the children were mostly Irish with some Polish and Italian ancestry, this French priest thought the adoptions would help heal divisions between Anglos and Mexicans in his new community.

Mandin asked Margarita Chacon, who had become his trusted assistant in just about everything, to help promote the adoptions in the parish. Mandin thought Margarita was Mexican because she spoke fluent Spanish as well as English. Actually, Margarita's parents had been German and English. She was born Margaret Miller and raised in a Catholic orphanage in El Paso.

Margarita came to church every day and stayed to help the young, inexperienced priest, who relied on her as a conduit of information to the community. She decorated the church, kept its records, supervised the cleaning, and held classes in catechism. She also taught reading and writing, both in English and Spanish, for Mexican children in her home.

Margarita, twenty-four, had been married six years to Cornelio Chacon, several years older. He had run away from Mexican peonage to raise himself to a good paying job in the smelter — good, anyway, for a Mexican at $2.25 a day. Anglos in the same job got more.

The Foundling Hospital believed in matching its children with their foster parents before the children left New York. Mandin had written that the list of families wanting to adopt "were not wealthy people, but all had work at good wages, had comfortable homes, were mostly childless, and could well take care of the little ones, and they were all good, practicing Catholics."

Of the forty children who arrived for adoption at Clifton-Morenci on October 1, 1904, Margarita and Cornelio had agreed to take two. Four-year-old Jerome Shanley had been born in a home for unwed mothers. His mother promptly disappeared, and a nurse took him to the Foundling Hospital when he was a month old. Three-year-old Katherine Fitzpatrick was born in the charity ward of a maternity hospital and lived with her mother for six months. Then the mother surrendered the baby to the Foundling Hospital.

The New York going-away clothing had been carefully folded and packed away for the seven-day, dusty, train trip — no bathing — so the children could meet their new families with an appearance matching their bright hopes. A few of the older ones like Jerome knew what a family was. The younger ones could sense from the Sisters of Charity that it was something wonderful.

As the train pulled into Clifton at 6:30 p. m. on Saturday, the sun had already disappeared behind the western peaks, deepening the haze from the smelter's smoke and fumes. But the children, newly dressed in their going-away best, were bright with anticipation.

The trouble began when the train stopped. The large crowd at the station included many Anglo women. Some may have come from curiosity, but others had the mistaken belief that they could select children right there. They had probably heard that some orphan trains operated that way, and they did not know about the Catholics matching their children with their families several weeks in advance.

When the Anglo women saw the children come off the train — the girls in their little white dresses and ribboned hair and the boys in sailor suits — they suddenly realized these were light-skinned Anglo children! Most had Irish faces, with blue eyes and some with red hair. The Anglo women could see that the Mexican women were expecting the orphans to become *their* children! After some near tugs of war over bewildered children and shouting matches with the Sisters, the Anglo women hurried home to carry the disturbing news to their husbands.

As Margarita walked to her home that evening, holding Jerome's hand and carrying Katherine, she knew the children were frightened from the crowd and the near altercations. She tried to assure them that coming to her home would be good for them as well as for her.

After several attempts, she and her husband had no living children, so Jerome and Katherine would be a great blessing to them. As a "mixed-race" woman who had been an orphan herself, Margarita expected to raise the children as true Americans, free from the separateness of class distinctions.

By Sunday morning the Anglo women had convinced their husbands a serious emergency existed, and it was necessary to rescue these Anglo children from their Mexican captors. Five of the husbands insisted that the Sheriff's office immediately arrest Father Mandin and George Swayne, the representative from the Foundling Hospital, who came with the children and the Sisters of Charity. Deputy Jeff Dunagan said he could not arrest without a warrant.

That afternoon the deputy and the Phelps Dodge superintendent met with the Sister in charge and told her the Mexicans did not make enough money to raise children, they didn't have beds to sleep in, and because of the "feeling" between the Anglos and the Mexicans, the children should be immediately reassigned to Anglos. The Sisters refused.

"It's a disgrace to the American people to place white children with people like these," the superintendent said.

"In that case," Swayne said, "I'm ashamed to be an American."

Soon a mob of four hundred had gathered in Morenci, many with guns. Several called for tar and feathers, some for a rope. The Sisters capitulated and agreed to take the children back from their new homes.

The return of the children did not quiet the crowd. One group of men rushed Father Mandin, knocked him to the ground and pummeled him with their fists. Later the priest fled, convinced he would be hanged.

That evening a crowd gathered in Clifton and traded stories about what they had heard regarding Catholic concern for orphan children. They said twenty children had died on the train from New York. Some had been given to Indians before they died. Catholics sold orphan children by the carload, like cattle. Mostly such children were the offspring of priests and nuns. Inflamed by such stories, and without waiting for any formal demand for the return of the children, they formed a posse to make the rescue. Bigotry, hatred, and vigilantism rode unchecked that rainy, Sunday night in Clifton.

On Monday Probate Judge P. C. Little arrived, and the Anglos asked him to issue adoption papers to them. When he tried to explain it was illegal without the consent of their legal guardian, the Foundling Hospital, the Anglos grew belligerent. Once again there was talk of tar and feathers and rope. At this time, the sixteen Clifton children were held by the

Anglos, and the Sisters had the other twenty-four in Morenci. Then Swayne and Mandin left town, leaving the seven Sisters of Charity to face the mob alone.

Before Swayne left he agreed that Deputy Dunagan, who had protected the children and the Sisters, could have two children in payment for his kindness. Dunagan gave the children to Anglos in Clifton who had failed to get any the night before. Then the mine superintendent said he knew a childless California doctor, visiting in Clifton, who wanted a child, and the Sisters released one to him.

The Sisters tried to reassure the released children that when the frenzy ended their new Anglo families would be good to them. But their deepest dread was for the souls of the Catholic children — now lost forever!

Then the mine superintendent, who now had the child he wanted to give his friend, told the crowd to go home. With his permission, the Sisters and the twenty-one, terrified, children remaining in their custody were allowed to return to New York.

The litigation over the sixteen children captured in Clifton was between the Foundling Hospital and the Anglos who claimed the children. No Mexican testified or was interviewed by a reporter or even sat in the audience at the trial before the Territorial Court. Mrs. Pascoe, who had taken Jerome Shanley, testified that she needed six weeks to get rid of the lice on his head. She was sure the lice came from the Mexicans during the few hours Margarita and Cornelio had him.

Muriel Wright, who had Katherine Fitzpatrick, testified that the Mexicans were illiterate, unclean, and spent all their earnings in drinking and gambling. The girl was brought in during the trial and placed on a desk. She laughed and waved her little hand at the court, and the judges gave up trying to keep down the crowd noise.

The Territorial Court decided for the Anglos, and the United States Supreme Court refused the petition filed to review the decision. The Anglos would keep the children they had acquired on that rain-filled, hate-filled night of terror!

Suggested reading: Linda Gordon, *The Great Arizona Orphan Abduction* (Cambridge: Harvard University, 1999).

ORDERING INFORMATION

True Tales of the Old West
is projected for 40 volumes.

For Titles in Print,
Ask at your bookstore
or write:

PIONEER PRESS
P. O. Box 216
Carson City, NV 89702-0216
(775) 888-9867
FAX (775) 888-0908

Other titles in progress include:

Frontier Artists
Army Women   Californios
Western Duelists   Early West Explorers
Government Leaders   Homesteaders
Early Lumbermen   Old West Merchants
Frontier Militiamen   Scientists & Engineers
Preachers & Spirit Guides   Frontier Teachers
Teamsters & Packers   Visitors to the Frontier
Doctors & Healers   Storms & Floods
Mysteries & Ghosts   Wild Animals